THE IMPORTANCE
OF LANGUAGE

2 . 00

THE IMPORTANCE
OF LANGUAGE

edited by Max Black

Cornell Paperbacks
Cornell University Press
Ithaca and London

First published 1962
First printing, Cornell Paperbacks, 1969
Second printing 1976
Published in the United Kingdom by Cornell University Press Ltd.,
2-4 Brook Street, London W1Y 1AA

International Standard Book Number 0-8014-9077-4
Library of Congress Catalog Card Number 62-13720
Printed in the United States of America

ACKNOWLEDGMENTS

The editor is grateful to the authors and publishers who have granted permission to reprint material from the following sources.

"Words and their Meanings." From a pamphlet with the same title by Aldous Huxley. Copyright 1940 by the Ward Ritchie Press. Reprinted by permission of the publishers.

"Thought and Language" by Samuel Butler was based on a lecture delivered in London, 1890. The present version is taken from *Collected Essays*, Vol. 2 of *The Shrewsbury Edition of the Works of Samuel Butler* (New York: E. P. Dutton & Co., Inc., 1925). Two initial paragraphs about the theory of evolution have been omitted.

"Bluspels and Flalansferes." From *Rehabilitations and Other Essays* by C. S. Lewis (London: Oxford University Press, 1939). Copyright 1939 by C. S. Lewis. Reprinted by permission of the author and Curtis Brown Ltd.

"Poetic Diction and Legal Fiction" by Owen Barfield. From *Essays Presented to Charles Williams* (London: Oxford University Press, 1947). Copyright 1947 by Owen Barfield. Reprinted by permission of the author and the Oxford University Press. I have omitted from the text the quotation of Walter de la Mare's poem, "Is there anybody there?"

"The Language of Magic." (Original title, "The General Theory of Magical Language.") From Vol. II of *Coral Gardens and Their Magic* by Bronislaw Malinowski. Copyright 1935 by George Allen & Unwin Ltd. Reprinted by permission of the publishers. A number of references to detailed illustrations in the book have been deleted.

"U and Non-U," by Alan S. C. Ross, first appeared under the title "Linguistic class-indicators in present-day English" in the Finnish philological journal *Neuphilologische Mitteilungen* (Helsinki, 1954). The present shortened and simplified version was published in *Noblesse Oblige,* Nancy Mitford, ed. (London: Hamish Hamilton Ltd., 1956). Copyright 1956 by Hamish Hamilton Ltd. Reprinted by permission of the publishers.

"The Resources of Language," by Friedrich Waismann, was originally published under the title of "Analytic-Synthetic V" (*Analysis*, XIII, October 1952). Copyright 1952 by *Analysis*. Reprinted by permission of the publishers. This was the fifth installment in a very long article which, after the sixth installment, remained unfinished.

"Essentially Contested Concepts" by W. B. Gallie. From the *Proceedings of the Aristotelian Society*, Vol. 56 (London, 1955-1956). Copyright 1956 by The Aristotelian Society. Reprinted by permission of the author and The Aristotelian Society.

"The Theory of Meaning" by Gilbert Ryle. From *British Philosophy in the Mid-Century*, C. A. Mace, ed. Copyright 1957 by George Allen & Unwin Ltd. Reprinted by permission of the publishers.

Words are the counters of wise men, but
the money of fools.

THOMAS HOBBES

Now it is not of fools exclusively, but
of the greater part of the thinking world,
that words are the money.

C. S. PEIRCE

Nothing is more common than for men
to think that because they are familiar
with words, they understand the ideas
they stand for.

J. H. NEWMAN

For all of us, grave or light, get our
thoughts entangled in metaphors, and
act fatally on the strength of them.

GEORGE ELIOT

FOREWORD

The essays that follow, all of which contain original and illuminating ideas about language, have appeared in places where they will be overlooked by the readers who would most enjoy them. In spite of an impressive amount of work on language by linguists, literary critics, psychologists, and philosophers, language still remains a marvel and a mystery. It remains wonderful that mere puffs of wind should allow men to discover what they think and feel, to share their attitudes and plans, to anticipate the future and learn from the past, and to create lasting works of art. One need only imagine the consequences of an onslaught of semantic amnesia, with progressive loss of meaning of the words we employ so casually, to be reminded of the importance of language in human affairs. Without words we would be dumb in more senses than one. Yet we understand very little, after centuries of investigation, about how this infinitely fine web of communication is established, improved, and preserved. We can be sure, however, that the old definition of language as a vehicle serving primarily for the expression and transmission of thought is too narrow to be helpful. All the essays that the reader is now invited to enjoy celebrate in their diverse ways the flexibility and versatility of language. And this, if I am not mistaken, is one of their chief merits.

M. B.

CONTENTS

THE IMPORTANCE
OF LANGUAGE

Words and Their Meanings

by ALDOUS HUXLEY

For a long time past, thinking men have tended to adopt a somewhat patronizing attitude towards the words they use in communicating with their fellows and formulating their own ideas. "What do you read, my lord?" Polonius asked. And with all the method that was in his madness Hamlet scornfully replied, "Words, words, words." That was at the beginning of the seventeenth century; and from that day to this the people who think themselves realists have gone on talking about words in the same contemptuous strain.

There was a reason for this behavior—or at least an excuse. Before the development of experimental science, words were too often regarded as having magical significance and power. With the rise of science a reaction set in, and for the last three centuries words have been unduly neglected as things having only the slightest importance. A great deal of attention has been paid, it is true, to the technical languages in which men of science do their specialized thinking, particularly, of course, to mathematics. But the colloquial usages of everyday speech, the literary and philosophical dialects in which men do their thinking about the problems of morals, politics, religion and psychology—these have been strangely neglected. We talk about "mere matters of words" in a tone which implies that we regard words as things beneath the notice of a serious-minded person.

This is a most unfortunate attitude. For the fact is that words play an enormous part in our lives and are therefore deserving of the closest study. The old idea that words possess magical powers is false; but its falsity is the distortion of a very important truth. Words *do* have a magical effect—but not in the way that the magicians supposed, and not on the objects they were trying to influence. Words are magical in the way they affect the minds of those who

use them. "A mere matter of words," we say contemptuously, for-
getting that words have power to mold men's thinking, to canalize
their feeling, to direct their willing and acting. Conduct and character are largely determined by the nature of the words we currently
use to discuss ourselves and the world around us. The magician is
a man who observes that words have an almost miraculous effect
on human behavior and who thinks that they must therefore be able
to exercise an equal power over inanimate nature. This tendency
to objectify psychological states and to project them, thus objectified,
into the external world is deeply rooted in the human mind. Men
have made this mistake in the past, men are making it now; and
the results are invariably deplorable. We owe to it not only the
tragic fooleries of black magic, but also (and this is even more
disastrous) most of the crimes and lunacies committed in the name
of religion, in the name of patriotism, in the name of political and
economic ideologies. In the age-long process by which men have
consistently stultified all their finest aspirations, words have played
a major part. It was, I believe, the realization of this fact that
prompted the founders of the two great world religions to insist
upon the importance of words. In the Christian gospels the reference
to this matter is contained in one of those brief and enigmatic
sayings which, like so many of the *logia,* unfortunately lend themselves to a great variety of interpretations. "But I say unto you, that
every idle word that men shall speak, they shall give account thereof
in the day of judgment. For by thy words thou shalt be justified,
and by thy words thou shalt be condemned." It is possible to interpret this utterance in terms of a merely magical theory of the significance of language. It is equally possible to put another construction
on the saying and to suppose that what Jesus was referring to was
what may be called the psychological magic of words, their power
to affect the thinking, feeling and behavior of those who use them.
That it was the intention of the Buddha to warn men against such
psychological magic the surviving documents leave us in no doubt
whatever. "Right speech" is one of the branches of the Buddhist's
Eightfold Path; and the importance of restraint in the use of words
for intellectual purposes is constantly stressed in all those passages in
the Pali Scriptures, where Gotama warns his followers against en-
tangling themselves in the chains of metaphysical argument.

It is time now to consider a little more closely the mechanism by
which words are able to exercise their psychological magic upon
the minds of men and women. Human beings are the inhabitants,
not of one universe, but of many universes. They are able to move

at will from the world, say, of atomic physics to the world of art, from the universe of discourse called "chemistry" to the universe of discourse called "ethics." Between these various universes philosophy and science have not as yet succeeded in constructing any bridges. How, for example, is an electron, or a chemical molecule, or even a living cell related to the G minor quintet of Mozart or the mystical theology of St. John of the Cross? Frankly, we don't know. We have no idea how thought and feeling are related to physical events in a living brain and only the very vaguest notions about the way in which a brain is related to the charges of electrical energy which appear to be its ultimate components. So far as we are concerned, the only connection between these various universes consists in the fact that we are able to talk about all of them and in some of them to have direct intuitions and sensuous experiences. The various universes we inhabit all belong to *us;* that is the only thing that unites them. Logical and scientific bridges are nonexistent; when we want to pass from one to another, we have to jump.

Now, all these various universes in which we live are members of one or other of two super-universes; the universe of direct experience and the universe of words. When I look at this paper in my hand I have a direct sensuous experience. If I choose to, I can keep my mouth shut and say nothing about this experience. Alternatively, I may open my mouth and, making use of a certain system of signs, called the English language, I may impart the information that my experience consisted of whiteness mitigated by rows of black marks which I recognize as belonging to the alphabetical system by means of which spoken language can be rendered in terms of a visible equivalent.

To discuss the formal mechanism by which the world of immediate human experience is related to the various languages of mankind is a task which, even if I had the time, I should be quite incompetent to perform. And fortunately it is not necessary for our present purposes that it should be performed. It is enough, in this context, to point out that, between the world of immediate experience and the world of language, between things and words, between events and speech, certain relations have in fact been established; and that these relations are governed by rules that are in part purely arbitrary, in part dictated by the nature of our common experiences. The form of the rules varies from language to language. We are not, however, concerned with these variations. For our present purposes, the significant fact is that all human societies use some kind of language and have done so from the remotest antiquity.

Human behavior as we know it, became possible only with the establishment of relatively stable systems of relationships between things and events on the one hand and words on the other. In societies where no such relationship has been established, that is to say, where there is no language, behavior is nonhuman. Necessarily so; for language makes it possible for men to build up the social heritage of accumulated skill, knowledge and wisdom, thanks to which it is possible for us to profit by the experiences of past generations, as though they were our own. There may be geniuses among the gorillas; but since gorillas have no conceptual language, the thoughts and achievements of these geniuses cannot be recorded and so are lost to simian posterity. In those limited fields of activity where some form of progress is possible, words permit of progress being made.

Nor is this all. The existence of language permits human beings to behave with a degree of purposefulness, perseverance and consistency unknown among the other mammals and comparable only to the purposefulness, perseverance and consistency of insects acting under the compulsive force of instinct. Every instant in the life, say, of a cat or a monkey tends to be irrelevant to every other instant. Such creatures are the victims of their moods. Each impulse as it makes itself felt carries the animal away completely. Thus, the urge to fight will suddenly be interrupted by the urge to eat; the all-absorbing passion of love will be displaced in the twinkling of an eye by a no less absorbing passion to search for fleas. The consistency of human behavior, such as it is, is due entirely to the fact that men have formulated their desires, and subsequently rationalized them, in terms of words. The verbal formulation of a desire will cause a man to go on pressing forward towards his goal, even when the desire itself lies dormant. Similarly, the rationalization of his desire in terms of some theological or philosophical system will convince him that he does well to persevere in this way. It is thanks to words and to words alone that, as the poet says:

Tasks in hours of insight willed
May be in hours of gloom fulfilled.

And let us remember incidentally that by no means all of our tasks are willed in hours of insight. Some are willed in hours of imbecility, some in hours of calculating self-interest; some under the stress of violent emotion, some in mere stupidity and intellectual confusion. If it were not for the descriptive and justificatory words with which we bind our days together, we should live like the animals in a series of discrete and separate spurts of impulse. From the psychological point of view, a theology or a philosophy may be defined as a device for permitting men to perform in cold blood and continuously actions which, otherwise, they could accomplish only by fits and starts and when the impulse was strong and hot within them. It is worth remarking, in this context, that no animals ever make war. They get into individual squabbles over food and sex; but they do not organize themselves in bands for the purpose of exterminating members of their own species in the name of some sacred cause. The emphasis here must be placed on the word "name." For, of course, animals have no lack of sacred causes. What could be more sacred to a tiger than fresh meat or tigresses? What is lacking in the animal's world is the verbal machinery for describing and justifying these sacred causes. Without words, perseverance and consistency of behavior are, as we have seen, impossible. And without perseverance in slaughter and consistency in hatred there can be no war.

For evil, then, as well as for good, words make us the human beings we actually are. Deprived of language we should be as dogs or monkeys. Possessing language, we are men and women able to persevere in crime no less than in heroic virtue, capable of intellectual achievements beyond the scope of any animal, but at the same time capable of systematic silliness and stupidity such as no dumb beast could ever dream of.

It is time now that I gave a few typical instances of the way in which words have power to modify men's thought, feeling and conduct. But before doing so, I must make a few more remarks of a general nature. For our present purposes, words may be divided into three main classes. The first class consists of words which designate definite and easily recognizable objects or qualities. Table, for example, is an easily recognizable object and brown an easily recognizable quality. Such words are unambiguous. No serious doubts as to their meaning exist. The second class contains words which designate entities and qualities less definite and less easily recognizable. Some of these are highly abstract words, generalizing certain features of many highly complex situations. Such words as "justice," "science," "society," are examples. In the same class we must place the numerous words which designate psychological states—words such as "beauty," "goodness," "spirit," "personality." I have already mentioned the apparently irresistible human tendency to objectify psychological states and project them, on the wings of their verbal

vehicle, into the outer world. Words like those I have just mentioned are typical vehicles of objectification. They are the cause of
endless intellectual confusion, endless emotional distress, endless
misdirections of voluntary effort.

Our third class contains words which are supposed to refer to
objects in the outer world or to psychological states, but which in
fact, since observation fails to reveal the existence of such objects or
states, refer only to figments of the imagination. Examples of such
words are the "dragon" of the Chinese and the "death instinct"
of Freudian psychologists.

The most effective, the most psychologically magical words are
found in the second category. This is only to be expected. Words
found in the second class are more ambiguous than any others and
can therefore be used in an almost indefinite number of contexts. A
recent American study has shown that the word "nature" has been
used by the philosophers of the West in no less than thirty-nine
distinct senses. The same philosopher will give it, all unconsciously
of course, three or four different meanings in as many paragraphs.
Given such ambiguity, any thesis can be defended, any course of
action morally justified, by an appeal to nature.

Ambiguity is not the only characteristic which makes these words
peculiarly effective in determining conduct. Those which stand for
generalizations and those which designate psychological states lend
themselves, as we have already seen, to objectification. They take
verbal wings and fly from the realm of abstraction into the realm of
the concrete, from the realm of psychology into the external universe.

The objectification and even the personification of abstractions is
something with which every political speech and newspaper article
has made us familiar. Nations are spoken of as though they were
persons having thoughts, feelings, a will and even a sex, which,
for some curious reason, is always female. This female, personal
nation produces certain psychological effects on those who hear it
(or rather her) being talked about—effects incomparably more violent than those that would be produced if politicians were to speak
about nations as what in fact they are: organized communities in-
habiting a certain geographical area and possessing the means to
wage war. This last point is crucially important. California is an
organized community; but since it does not possess an army and
navy, it cannot qualify for a place in the League of Nations.

Another familiar entity in political speeches is the pseudo-person
called "Society." Society has a will, thoughts and feelings, but, unlike

the Nation, no sex. The most cursory observation suffices to show that there is no such thing as Society with a large S. There are only very large numbers of individual societies, organized in different ways for different purposes. The issue is greatly complicated by the fact that the people who talk about this nonexistent Society with a big S, tend to do so in terms of biological analogies which are, in many cases, wholly inapplicable. For example, the so-called philosophical historians insist on talking of a society as though it were an organism. In some aspects, perhaps, a society does resemble an organism. In others, however, it certainly does not. Organisms grow old and die and their component cells break down into inanimate substances. This does not happen to a society, though many historians and publicists loosely talk as though it did. The individuals who compose what is called a decadent or collapsed society do not break down into carbon and water. They remain alive; but the cells of a dead organism are dead and have ceased to be cells and become something else. If we want to talk about the decline and fall of societies in terms of scientific analogies, we had better choose our analogy from physics rather than biology. A given quantity of water, for example, will show least energy, more energy, most energy according to its temperature. It has most energy in the form of superheated steam, least in the form of ice. Similarly, a given society will exhibit much energy or little energy according to the way in which its individual members live their lives. The society of Roman Italy, for example, did not die; it passed from a high state of energy to a lower state of energy. It is for historians to determine the physiological, psychological, economic and religious conditions accompanying respectively a high and a low degree of social energy.

The tendency to objectify and personify abstractions is found not only among politicians and newspaper men, but also among those who belong to the, intellectually speaking, more respectable classes of the community. By way of example, I shall quote a paragraph from the address delivered by Clerk Maxwell to the British Association in 1873. Clerk Maxwell was one of the most brilliantly original workers in the whole history of physics. He was also what many scientists, alas, are not—a highly cultivated man capable of using his intelligence in fields outside his particular specialty. Here is what he could say before a learned society, when at the height of his powers.

"No theory of evolution," he wrote, "can be formed to account for the similarity of molecules." (Throughout this passage, Maxwell is using the word "molecule" in the sense in which we should now use the word "atom.") "For evolution necessarily implies continuous change, and the molecule is incapable of growth or decay, of generation or destruction. None of the processes of Nature, from the time when Nature began, have produced the slightest difference in the properties of any molecule. We are therefore unable to ascribe either the existence of the molecules or the identity of their properties to any of the causes which we call natural. Thus we have been led along a strictly scientific path very near to the point at which Science must stop. . . . In tracing back the history of matter Science is arrested when she assures herself, on the one hand that the molecule has been made and, on the other, that it has not been made by any of the processes which we call natural."

The most interesting point that emerges from these lines is the fact that, like the Nation, but unlike Society, Science has a sex and is a female. Having recorded this item in our text books of natural history, we can go on to study the way in which even a mind of the caliber of Clerk Maxwell's can be led into absurdity by neglecting to analyze the words which it uses to express itself. The word "science" is current in our everyday vocabulary. It can be spelt with a capital S. Therefore it can be thought of as a person; for the names of persons are always spelt with capital letters. A person who is called Science must, *ex hypothesi,* be infallible. This being so, she can pronounce without risk of contradiction, that "none of the processes of Nature, since the time when Nature began," (Nature is also spelt with a capital letter and is of course also a female) "have produced the slightest difference in the properties of any molecule." Twenty-three years after the date of Maxwell's speech, Becquerel observed the radioactivity of uranium. Two years after that Mme. Curie discovered radium. At the turn of the new century Rutherford and Soddy demonstrated the fact that the radium atom was in a process of rapid disintegration and was itself derived from uranium whose atoms were disintegrating at a much slower rate.

This cautionary story shows how fatally easy it is for even the greatest men of science to take the particular ignorance of their own time and place, and raise it to the level of a universal truth of nature. Such errors are particularly easy when words are used in the entirely illegitimate way in which Maxwell employed the word "Science." What Maxwell should have said was something like this, "Most Western scientists in the year 1873 believe that no process has ever modified the internal structure of individual atoms. If this is so (and of course the beliefs of 1873 may have to be modified at any moment in the light of new discoveries), then perhaps it may be legitimate to draw certain inferences of a theological nature regarding the creation of matter."

How was it possible, we may ask ourselves, that a man of Clerk Maxwell's prodigious intellectual powers, should have committed a blunder so monstrously ridiculous, so obvious, when attention is called to it, to people of even the most ordinary mental capacities? The question demands a double answer—the first on the purely intellectual level, the second in terms of feeling and will. Let us deal with these in order. Maxwell made his mistake, first of all, out of a genuine intellectual confusion. He had accepted the English language without question or analysis, as a fish accepts the water it lives in. This may seem curious in the light of the fact that he had certainly not accepted the technical language of mathematics without question or analysis. We must remember, however, that nontechnical language is picked up in infancy, by imitation, by trial and error, much as the arts of walking and rudimentary cleanliness are acquired. Technical languages are learned at a later period in life, are applied only in special situations where analysis is regarded as creditable and the ordinary habits of daily living are in abeyance. Children and young people must be deliberately taught to analyze the nontechnical language of daily life. With very few exceptions, they will never undertake the task on their own initiative. In this respect, Maxwell was not exceptional. He turned his intensely original and powerful mind on to the problems of physics and mathematics, but never on those of everyday, untechnical language. This he took as he found it. And as he found in it such words as "Science" with a capital S and a female sex, he made use of them. The results, as we have seen, were disastrous.

The second reason for Maxwell's error was evidently of an emotional and voluntary nature. He had been piously brought up in the Protestant tradition. He was also, as the few letters to his wife which have been printed seem to indicate, a practising mystic. In announcing that "Science" with the capital S and the female sex had proved that atoms had not evolved, but had been created and kept unchangingly themselves by nonnatural forces, he had a specifically religious purpose in view. He wanted to show that the existence of a demiurge after the pattern of Jehovah, could be demonstrated scientifically. And he wanted also, I suspect, to prove to himself that the psychological states into which he entered during his moments of mystical experience could be objectified and personified in the form of the Hebraic deity, in whose existence he had been taught to believe during childhood.

This brings us to the threshold of a subject, profoundly interesting indeed, but so vast that I must not even attempt to discuss it here; the subject of God and of the relations subsisting between that word and the external world of things and events, between that word and the inner world of psychological states. Shelley has sketched the nature of the problem in a few memorable sentences. "The thoughts which the word, 'God,' suggests to the human mind are susceptible of as many varieties as human minds themselves. The Stoic, the Platonist and the Epicurean, the Polytheist, the Dualist and the Trinitarian, differ infinitely in their conceptions of its meaning. . . . And not only has every sect distinct conceptions of the application of this name, but scarcely two individuals of the same sect, who exercise in any degree the freedom of their judgment, or yield themselves with any candor of feeling to the influencings of the visible world, find perfect coincidence of opinion to exist between them." Such, I repeat, is the problem. No complete solution of it is possible. But it can at least be very considerably clarified by anyone who is prepared to approach it armed with equipment suitable to deal with it. What is the nature of this suitable equipment? I would assign the first place to an adequate vocabulary. Students of religion have need of a language sufficiently copious and sufficiently analytical to make it possible for them to distinguish between the various types of religious experience, to recognize the difference between things and words, and to realize when they are objectifying psychological states and projecting them into the outside world. Lacking such a language they will find that even a wide knowledge in the fields of theology, of comparative religion and of human behavior will be of little use to them. It will be of little use for the simple reason that such knowledge has been recorded, up to the present time, in words that lend themselves to the maximum amount of intellectual confusion and the minimum of clarity and distinctness.

Words and their meanings—the subject is an enormous one. "Had we but world enough and time" as the poet says, we could continue our discussion of it almost indefinitely. But unfortunately, or perhaps fortunately, world and time are lacking, and I must draw to a close. I have been able in this place to let fall only a few casual and unsystematic remarks about those particular aspects of the science of signs which Charles Morris has called the semantic and pragmatic dimensions of general semiosis. I hope, however, that I have said enough to arouse an interest in the subject, to evoke in your minds a sense of its profound importance and a realization of the need to incorporate it systematically into the educational curriculum.

Any education that aims at completeness must be at once theoretical and practical, intellectual and moral. Education in the proper use of words is complete in the sense that it is not merely intellectual and theoretical. Those who teach, teach not only the science of signs, but also a universally useful art and a most important moral discipline. The proper use of language is an important moral discipline, for the good reason that, in this field as in all others, most mistakes have a voluntary origin. We commit intellectual blunders because it suits our interests to do so, or because our blunders are of such a nature that we get pleasure or excitement from committing them. I have pointed out that one of the reasons for Maxwell's really monstrous misuse of language must be sought in that great man's desire to reconcile his scientific ideas with the habits of religious belief he had contracted in childhood. There was a genuine confusion of thought; but a not entirely creditable wish was very definitely the father of this confusion. And the same is true, of course, about those who for propagandist purposes, personify such abstractions as "Society" or "the Nation." A wish is father to their mistaken thought—the wish to influence their hearers to act in the way they would like them to act. Similarly, a wish is the father of the mistaken thought of those who allow themselves to be influenced by such preposterous abuses of language—the wish to be excited, to "get a kick," as the phrase goes. Objectified in the form of a person, the idea of a nation can arouse much stronger feelings than it can evoke when it is spoken of in more sober and accurate language. The poor fools who, as we like to think, are helplessly led astray by such machiavellian demagogues as Hitler and Mussolini are led astray because they get a lot of emotional fun out of being bamboozled in this way. We shall find, upon analysis, that very many of the intellectual errors committed by us in our use of words have a similar emotional or voluntary origin. To learn to use words correctly is to learn, among other things, the art of foregoing immediate excitements and immediate personal triumphs. Much self control and great disinterestedness are needed by those who would realize the ideal of never misusing language. Moreover, a man who habitually speaks and writes correctly is one who has cured himself, not merely of conscious and deliberate lying, but also (and the task is much more difficult and at least as important) of unconscious mendacity. When Gotama insisted on Right Speech, when Jesus stressed the significance of every idle word, they were not lecturing on the theory of semiosis; they were inculcating the practice of the highest virtues. Words and the meanings of words are not matters merely for the academic amusement of linguists and logisticians, or for the aesthetic delight of poets; they are matters of the profoundest ethical significance to every human being.

Thought and Language

by SAMUEL BUTLER

It may perhaps be expected that I should begin a lecture on the relations between thought and language with some definition of both these things; but thought, as Sir William Grove said of motion, is a phenomenon "so obvious to simple apprehension that to define it would make it more obscure." [1] Definitions are useful where things are new to us, but they are superfluous about those that are already familiar, and mischievous, so far as they are possible at all, in respect of all those things that enter so profoundly and intimately into our being that in them we must either live or bear no life. To vivisect the more vital processes of thought is to suspend, if not to destroy them; for thought can think about everything more healthily and easily than about itself. It is like its instrument the brain, which knows nothing of any injuries inflicted upon itself. As regards what is new to us, a definition will sometimes dilute a difficulty, and help us to swallow that which might choke us un-diluted; but to define when we have once well swallowed is to un-settle, rather than settle, our digestion. Definitions, again, are like steps cut in a steep slope of ice, or shells thrown on to a greasy pavement; they give us foothold, and enable us to advance, but when we are at our journey's end we want them no longer. Again, they are useful as mental fluxes, and as helping us to fuse new ideas with our older ones. They present us with some tags and ends of ideas that we have already mastered, on to which we can hitch our new ones; but to multiply them in respect of such a matter as thought, is like scratching the bite of a gnat; the more we scratch the more we want to scratch; the more we define the more we shall have to go on defining the words we have used in our definitions, and shall end by setting up a serious mental raw in the place of a

[1] Sir William Grove, *Correlation of Forces* (New York: Longmans, Green & Co., Inc., 1874), p. 15.

small uneasiness that was after all quite endurable. We know too well what thought is, to be able to know that we know it, and I am persuaded there is no one in this room but understands what is meant by thought and thinking well enough for all the purposes of this discussion. Whoever does not know this without words will not learn it for all the words and definitions that are laid before him. The more, indeed, he hears, the more confused he will become. I shall, therefore, merely premise that I use the word "thought" in the same sense as that in which it is generally used by people who say that they think this or that. At any rate, it will be enough if I take Professor Max Müller's own definition, and say that its essence consists in a bringing together of mental images and ideas with deductions therefrom, and with a corresponding power of detaching them from one another. Hobbes, the Professor tells us, maintained this long ago, when he said that all our thinking consists of addition and subtraction—that is to say, in bringing ideas together, and in detaching them from one another.

Turning from thought to language, we observe that the word is derived from the French *langue*, or "tongue." Strictly, therefore, it means "tonguage." This, however, takes account of but a very small part of the ideas that underlie the word. It does, indeed, seize a familiar and important detail of everyday speech, though it may be doubted whether the tongue has more to do with speaking than lips, teeth, and throat have, but it makes no attempt at grasping and expressing the essential characteristic of speech. Anything done with the tongue, even though it involve no speaking at all, is "tonguage"; eating oranges is as much tonguage as speech is. The word, therefore, though it tells us in part how speech is effected, reveals nothing of that ulterior meaning which is nevertheless inseparable from any right use of the words either "speech" or "language." It presents us with what is indeed a very frequent adjunct of conversation, but the use of written characters, or the finger-speech of deaf mutes. is enough to show that the word "language" omits all reference to the most essential characteristics of the idea, which in practice it nevertheless very sufficiently presents to us. I hope presently to make it clear to you how and why it should do so. The word is incomplete in the first place, because it omits all reference to the ideas which words, speech, or language are intended to convey, and there can be no true word without its actually or potentially conveying an idea. Secondly, it makes no allusion to the person or persons to whom the ideas are to be conveyed. Language is not language unless it not only expresses fairly definite and coherent ideas, but unless it also conveys these ideas to some other living intelligent being, either man or brute, that can understand them. We may speak to a dog or horse, but not to a stone. If we make pretence of doing so we are in reality only talking to ourselves. The person or animal spoken to is half the battle—a half, moreover, which is essential to there being any battle at all. It takes two people to say a thing—a sayee as well as a sayer. The one is as essential to any true saying as the other. A. may have spoken, but if B. has not heard there has been nothing said, and he must speak again. True, the belief on A.'s part that he had a *bona fide* sayee in B., saves his speech *qua* him, but it has been barren and left no fertile issue. It has failed to fulfil the conditions of true speech, which involve not only that A. should speak, but also that B. should hear. True, again, we often speak of loose, incoherent, indefinite language; but by doing so we imply, and rightly, that we are calling that language which is not true language at all. People, again, sometimes talk to themselves without intending that any other person should hear them, but this is not well done, and does harm to those who practise it. It is abnormal, whereas our concern is with normal and essential characteristics; we may, therefore, neglect both delirious babblings, and the cases in which a person is regarding him or herself, as it were, from outside, and treating himself as though he were someone else.

Inquiring, then, what are the essentials, the presence of which constitutes language, while their absence negatives it altogether, we find that Professor Max Müller restricts them to the use of grammatical articulate words that we can write or speak, and denies that anything can be called language unless it can be written or spoken in articulate words and sentences. He also denies that we can think at all unless we do so in words; that is to say, in sentences with verbs and nouns. Indeed, he goes so far as to say upon his title page that there can be no reason—which I imagine comes to much the same thing as thought—without language, and no language without reason.

Against the assertion that there can be no true language without reason I have nothing to say. But when the Professor says that there can be no reason, or thought, without language, his opponents contend, as it seems to me, with greater force, that thought, though infinitely aided, extended and rendered definite through the invention of words, nevertheless existed so fully as to deserve no other name thousands, if not millions, of years before words had entered into it at all. Words, they say, are a comparatively recent invention, for the fuller expression of something that was already in existence.

Children, they urge, are often evidently thinking and reasoning, though they can neither think nor speak in words. If you ask me to define reason, I answer as before that this can no more be done than thought, truth, or motion can be defined. Who has answered the question, "What is truth?" Man cannot see God and live. We cannot go so far back upon ourselves as to undermine our own foundations; if we try to do so we topple over, and lose that very reason about which we vainly try to reason. If we let the foundations be, we know well enough that they are there, and we can build upon them in all security. We cannot, then, define reason nor crib, cabin, and confine it within a thus-far-shalt-thou-go-and-no-farther. Who can define heat or cold, or night or day? Yet, so long as we hold fast by current consent, our chances of error for want of better definition are so small that no sensible person will consider them. In like manner, if we hold by current consent or common sense, which is the same thing, about reason, we shall not find the want of an academic definition hinder us from a reasonable conclusion. What nurse or mother will doubt that her infant child can reason within the limits of its own experience, long before it can formulate its reason in articulately worded thought? If the development of any given animal is, as our opponents themselves admit, an epitome of the history of its whole anterior development, surely the fact that speech is an accomplishment acquired after birth so artificially that children who have gone wild in the woods lose it if they have ever learned it, points to the conclusion that man's ancestors only learned to express themselves in articulate language at a comparatively recent period. Granted that they learn to think and reason continually the more and more fully for having done so, will common sense permit us to suppose that they could neither think not reason at all till they could convey their ideas in words?

I will return later to the reason of the lower animals, but will now deal with the question what it is that constitutes language in the most comprehensive sense that can be properly attached to it. I have said already that language to be language at all must not only convey fairly definite coherent ideas, but must also convey them to another living being. Whenever two living beings have conveyed and received ideas, there has been language, whether looks or gestures or words spoken or written have been the vehicle by means of which the ideas have travelled. Some ideas crawl, some run, some fly; and in this case words are the wings they fly with, but they are only the wings of thought or of ideas, they are not the thought or ideas themselves, nor yet, as Professor Max Müller would have it, inseparably connected with them. Last summer I was at an inn in Sicily, where there was a deaf and dumb waiter; he had been born so, and could neither write nor read. What had he to do with words or words with him? Are we to say, then, that this most active, amiable, and intelligent fellow could neither think nor reason? One day I had had my dinner and had left the hotel. A friend came in, and the waiter saw him look for me in the place I generally occupied. He instantly came up to my friend and moved his two forefingers in a way that suggested two people going about together, this meant "your friend"; he then moved his forefingers horizontally across his eyes, this meant, "who wears divided spectacles"; he made two fierce marks over the sockets of his eyes, this meant, "with the heavy eyebrows"; he pulled his chin, and then touched his white shirt, to say that my beard was white. Having thus identified me as a friend of the person he was speaking to, and as having a white beard, heavy eyebrows, and wearing divided spectacles, he made a munching movement with his jaws to say that I had had my dinner; and finally, by making two fingers imitate walking on the table, he explained that I had gone away. My friend, however, wanted to know how long I had been gone, so he pulled out his watch and looked inquiringly. The man at once slapped himself on the back, and held up the five fingers of one hand, to say it was five minutes ago. All this was done as rapidly as though it had been said in words; and my friend, who knew the man well, understood without a moment's hesitation. Are we to say that this man had no thought, nor reason, nor language, merely because he had not a single word of any kind in his head, which I am assured he had not; for, I should add, he could not speak with his fingers? Is it possible to deny that a dialogue—an intelligent conversation—had passed between the two men? And if conversation, then surely it is technical and pedantic to deny that all the essential elements of language were present. The signs and tokens used by this poor fellow were as rude an instrument of expression, in comparison with ordinary language, as going on one's hands and knees is in comparison with walking, or as walking compared with going by train; but it is as great an abuse of words to limit the word "language" to mere words written or spoken, as it would be to limit the idea of a locomotive to a railway engine. This may indeed pass in ordinary conversation, where so much must be suppressed if talk is to be got through at all, but it is intolerable when we are inquiring about the relations between thought and words. To do so is to let words become as it were the masters of thought, on the ground that the fact of their being only

its servants and appendages is so obvious that it is generally allowed
to go without saying.

If all that Professor Max Müller means to say is, that no animal
but man commands an articulate language, with verbs and nouns,
or is ever likely to command one (and I question whether in reality
he means much more than this), no one will differ from him. No
dog or elephant has one word for bread, another for meat, and another for water. Yet, when we watch a cat or dog dreaming, as they
often evidently do, can we doubt that the dream is accompanied
by a mental image of the thing that is dreamed of, much like what
we experience in dreams ourselves, and much doubtless like the
mental images which must have passed through the mind of my
deaf and dumb waiter? If they have mental images in sleep, can we
doubt that waking, also, they picture things before their mind's
eyes, and see them much as we do—too vaguely indeed to admit of
our thinking that we actually see the objects themselves, but definitely enough for us to be able to recognize the idea or object of
which we are thinking, and to connect it with any other idea, object,
or sign that we may think appropriate?

Here we have touched on the second essential element of language.
We laid it down, that its essence lay in the communication of an
idea from one intelligent being to another; but no ideas can be
communicated at all except by the aid of conventions to which both
parties have agreed to attach an identical meaning. The agreement
may be very informal, and may pass so unconsciously from one generation to another that its existence can only be recognized by the
aid of much introspection, but it will be always there. A sayer, a
sayee, and a convention, no matter what, agreed upon between them
as inseparably attached to the idea which it is intended to convey—
these comprise all the essentials of language. Where these are present
there is language; where any of them are wanting there is no language. It is not necessary for the sayee to be able to speak and become a sayer. If he comprehends the sayer—that is to say, if he
attaches the same meaning to a certain symbol as the sayer does—if
he is a party to the bargain whereby it is agreed upon by both that
any given symbol shall be attached invariably to a certain idea, so
that in virtue of the principle of associated ideas the symbol shall
never be present without immediately carrying the idea along with
it, then all the essentials of language are complied with, and there
has been true speech though never a word was spoken.

The lower animals, therefore, many of them, possess a part of our own language, though they cannot speak it, and hence do not possess it so fully as we do. They cannot say "bread," "meat," or "water," but there are many that readily learn what ideas they ought to attach to these symbols when they are presented to them. It is idle to say that a cat does not know what the cat's-meat man means when he says "meat." The cat knows just as well, neither better nor worse than the cat's-meat man does, and a great deal better than I myself understand much that is said by some very clever people at Oxford or Cambridge. There is more true employment of language, more *bona fide* currency of speech, between a sayer and a sayee who understand each other, though neither of them can speak a word, than between a sayer who can speak with the tongues of men and of angels without being clear about his own meaning, and a sayee who can himself utter the same words, but who is only in imperfect agreement with the sayer as to the ideas which the words or symbols that he utters are intended to convey. The nature of the symbols counts for nothing; the gist of the matter is in the perfect harmony between sayer and sayee as to the significance that is to be associated with them.

Professor Max Müller admits that we share with the lower animals what he calls an emotional language, and continues that we may call their interjections and imitations language if we like, as we speak of the language of the eyes or the eloquence of mute nature, but he warns us against mistaking metaphor for fact. It is indeed mere metaphor to talk of the eloquence of mute nature, or the language of winds and waves. There is no intercommunion of mind with mind by means of a covenanted symbol; but it is only an apparent, not a real, metaphor to say that two pairs of eyes have spoken when they have signalled to one another something which they both understand. A schoolboy at home for the holidays wants another plate of pudding, and does not like to apply officially for more. He catches the servant's eye and looks at the pudding; the servant understands, takes his plate without a word, and gets him some. Is it metaphor to say that the boy asked the servant to do this, or is it not rather pedantry to insist on the letter of a bond and deny its spirit, by denying that language passed, on the ground that the symbols covenanted upon and assented to by both were uttered and received by eyes and not by mouth and ears? When the lady drank to the gentleman only with her eyes, and he pledged with his, was there no conversation because there was neither noun nor verb? Eyes are verbs, and glasses of wine are good nouns enough

as between those who understand one another. Whether the ideas
underlying them are expressed and conveyed by eyeage or by tonguage is a detail that matters nothing.

But everything we say is metaphorical if we choose to be captious.
Scratch the simplest expressions, and you will find the metaphor.
Written words are handage, inkage, and paperage; it is only by
metaphor, or substitution and transposition of ideas, that we can
call them language. They are indeed potential language, and the
symbols employed presuppose nouns, verbs, and the other parts of
speech; but for the most part it is in what we read between the lines
that the profounder meaning of any letter is conveyed. There are
words unwritten and untranslatable into any nouns that are nevertheless felt as above, about, and underneath the gross material symbols that lie scrawled upon the paper; and the deeper the feeling
with which anything is written the more pregnant will it be of
meaning which can be conveyed securely enough, but which loses
rather than gains if it is squeezed into a sentence, and limited by
the parts of speech. The language is not in the words but in the
heart-to-heartness of the thing, which is helped by words, but is
nearer and farther than they. A correspondent wrote to me once,
many years ago, "If I could think to you without words you would
understand me better." But surely in this he was thinking to me,
and without words, and I did understand him better. . . . So it is
not by the words that I am too presumptuously venturing to speak
tonight that your opinions will be formed or modified. They will be
formed or modified, if either, by something that you will feel, but
which I have not spoken, to the full as much as by anything that
I have actually uttered. You may say that this borders on mysticism.
Perhaps it does, but there really is some mysticism in nature.

To return, however, to *terra firma*. I believe I am right in saying
that the essence of language lies in the intentional conveyance of
ideas from one living being to another through the instrumentality
of arbitrary tokens or symbols agreed upon and understood by both
as being associated with the particular ideas in question. The nature
of the symbol chosen is a matter of indifference; it may be anything
that appeals to human senses, and is not too hot or too heavy; the
essence of the matter lies in a mutual covenant that whatever it is
shall stand invariably for the same thing, or nearly so.

We shall see this more easily if we observe the differences between
written and spoken language. The written word "stone," and the
spoken word, are each of them symbols arrived at in the first instance

arbitrarily. They are neither of them more like the other than they are to the idea of a stone which rises before our minds, when we either see or hear the word, or than this idea again is like the actual stone itself, but nevertheless the spoken symbol and the written one each alike convey with certainty the combination of ideas to which we have agreed to attach them.

The written symbol is formed with the hand, appeals to the eye, leaves a material trace as long as paper and ink last, can travel as far as paper and ink can travel, and can be imprinted on eye after eye practically *ad infinitum* both as regards time and space.

The spoken symbol is formed by means of various organs in or about the mouth, appeals to the ear, not the eye, perishes instantly without material trace, and if it lives at all does so only in the minds of those who heard it. The range of its action is no wider than that within which a voice can be heard; and every time a fresh impression is wanted the type must be set up anew.

The written symbol extends infinitely, as regards time and space, the range within which one mind can communicate with another; it gives the writer's mind a life limited by the duration of ink, paper, and readers, as against that of his flesh and blood body. On the other hand, it takes longer to learn the rules so as to be able to apply them with ease and security, and even then they cannot be applied so quickly and easily as those attaching to spoken symbols. Moreover, the spoken symbols admit of a hundred quick and subtle adjuncts by way of action, tone, and expression, so that no one will use written symbols unless either for the special advantages of permanence and travelling power, or because he is incapacitated from using spoken ones. This, however, is hardly to the point; the point is that these two conventional combinations of symbols, that are as unlike one another as the Hallelujah Chorus is to St. Paul's Cathedral, are the one as much language as the other; and we therefore inquire what this very patent fact reveals to us about the more essential characteristics of language itself. What is the common bond that unites these two classes of symbols that seem at first sight to have nothing in common, and makes the one raise the idea of language in our minds as readily as the other? The bond lies in the fact that both are a set of conventional tokens or symbols, agreed upon between the parties to whom they appeal as being attached invariably to the same ideas, and because they are being made as a means of communion between one mind and another—for a memorandum made for a person's own later use is nothing but a communi-

cation from an earlier mind to a later and modified one; it is therefore in reality a communication from one mind to another as much
as though it had been addressed to another person.

We see, therefore, that the nature of the outward and visible sign
to which the inward and spiritual idea of language is attached does
not matter. It may be the firing of a gun; it may be an old semaphore
telegraph; it may be the movements of a needle; a look, a gesture,
the breaking of a twig by an Indian to tell someone that he has
passed that way: a twig broken designedly with this end in view is
a letter addressed to whomsoever it may concern, as much as though
it had been written out in full on bark or paper. It does not matter
one straw what it is, provided it is agreed upon in concert, and
stuck to. Just as the lowest forms of life nevertheless present us with
all the essential characteristics of livingness, and are as much alive
in their own humble way as the most highly developed organisms,
so the rudest intentional and effectual communication between two
minds through the instrumentality of a concerted symbol is as much
language as the most finished oratory of Mr. Gladstone. I demur
therefore to the assertion that the lower animals have no language,
inasmuch as they cannot themselves articulate a grammatical sentence. I do not indeed pretend that when the cat calls upon the tiles
it uses what it consciously and introspectively recognizes as language;
it says what it has to say without introspection, and in the ordinary
course of business, as one of the common forms of courtship. It no
more knows that it has been using language than M. Jourdain knew
he had been speaking prose, but M. Jourdain's knowing or not
knowing was neither here nor there.

Anything which can be made to hitch on invariably to a definite
idea that can carry some distance—say an inch at the least, and
which can be repeated at pleasure, can be pressed into the service of
language. Mrs. Bentley, wife of the famous Dr. Bentley of Trinity
College, Cambridge, used to send her snuff-box to the college buttery
when she wanted beer, instead of a written order. If the snuff-box
came the beer was sent, but if there was no snuff-box there was no
beer. Wherein did the snuff-box differ more from a written order,
than a written order differs from a spoken one? The snuff-box was
for the time being language. It sounds strange to say that one might
take a pinch of snuff out of a sentence, but if the servant had helped
him or herself to a pinch while carrying it to the buttery this is what
would have been done; for if a snuff-box can say "Send me a quart
of beer," so efficiently that the beer is sent, it is impossible to say
that it is not a *bona fide* sentence. As for the recipient of the mes-

sage, the butler did not probably translate the snuff-box into articulate nouns and verbs; as soon as he saw it he just went down into the cellar and drew the beer, and if he thought at all, it was probably about something else. Yet he must have been thinking without words, or he would have drawn too much beer or too little, or have spilt it in the bringing it up, and we may be sure that he did none of these things.

You will, of course, observe that if Mrs. Bentley had sent the snuff-box to the buttery of St. John's College instead of Trinity, it would not have been language, for there would have been no covenant between sayer and sayee as to what the symbol should represent, there would have been no previously established association of ideas in the mind of the butler of St. John's between beer and snuff-box; the connection was artificial, arbitrary, and by no means one of those in respect of which an impromptu bargain **might** be proposed by the very symbol itself, and assented to without previous formality by the person to whom it was presented. More briefly, the butler of St. John's would not have been able to understand and read it aright. It would have been a dead letter to him—a snuff-box and not a letter; whereas to the butler of Trinity it was a letter and not a snuff-box. You will also note that it was only at the moment when he was looking at it and accepting it as a message that it flashed forth from snuff-box hood into the light and life of living utterance. As soon as it had kindled the butler into sending a single quart of beer, its force was spent until Mrs. Bentley threw her soul into it again and charged it anew by wanting more beer, and sending it down accordingly.

Again, take the ring which the Earl of Essex sent to Queen Elizabeth, but which the queen did not receive. This was intended as a sentence, but failed to become effectual language because the sensible material symbol never reached those sentient organs which it was intended to affect. A book, again, however full of excellent words it may be, is not language when it is merely standing on a bookshelf. It speaks to no one, unless when being actually read, or quoted from by an act of memory. It is potential language as a lucifer-match is potential fire, but it is no more language till it is in contact with a recipient mind, than a match is fire till it is struck, and is being consumed.

A piece of music, again, without any words at all, or a song with words that have nothing in the world to do with the ideas which it is nevertheless made to convey, is very often effectual language. Much lying, and all irony depends on tampering with covenanted symbols, and making those that are usually associated with one set of ideas convey by a sleight of mind others of a different nature. That is why irony is intolerably fatiguing unless very sparingly used. Take the song which Blondel sang under the window of King Richard's prison. There was not one syllable in it to say that Blondel was there, and was going to help the king to get out of prison. It was about some silly love affair, but it was a letter all the same, and the king made language of what would otherwise have been no language, by guessing the meaning, that is to say, by perceiving that he was expected to enter then and there into a new covenant as to the meaning of the symbols that were presented to him, understanding what this covenant was to be, and acquiescing in it.

On the other hand, no ingenuity can torture "language" into being a fit word to use in connection with either sounds or any other symbols that have not been intended to convey a meaning, or again in connection with either sounds or symbols in respect of which there has been no covenant between sayer and sayee. When we hear people speaking a foreign language—we will say Welsh—we feel that though they are no doubt using what is very good language as between themselves, there is no language whatever as far as we are concerned. We call it lingo, not language. The Chinese letters on a tea-chest might as well not be there, for all that they say to us, though the Chinese find them very much to the purpose. They are a covenant to which we have been no parties—to which our intelligence has affixed no signature.

We have already seen that it is in virtue of such an understood covenant that symbols so unlike one another as the written word "stone" and the spoken word alike at once raise the idea of a stone in our minds. See how the same holds good as regards the different languages that pass current in different nations. The letters p, i, e, r, r, e convey the idea of a stone to a Frenchman as readily as s, t, o, n, e do to ourselves. And why? because that is the covenant that has been struck between those who speak and those who are spoken to. Our "stone" conveys no idea to a Frenchman, nor his "pierre" to us, unless we have done what is commonly called acquiring one another's language. To acquire a foreign language is only to learn and adhere to the covenants in respect of symbols which the nation in question has adopted and adheres to. Till we have done this we neither of us know the rules, so to speak, of the game that the other is playing, and cannot, therefore, play together; but the convention being once known and consented to, it does not matter whether we raise the idea of a stone by the words "lapis," or by "lithos," "pietra," "pierre," "stein," "stane," or "stone"; we may choose what symbols written or spoken we choose, and one set, unless they are of unwieldly length, will do as well as another, if we can get other people to choose the same and stick to them; it is the accepting and sticking to them that matters, not the symbols. The whole power of spoken language is vested in the invariableness with which certain symbols are associated with certain ideas. If we are strict in always connecting the same symbols with the same ideas, we speak well, keep our meaning clear to ourselves, and convey it readily and accurately to anyone who is also fairly strict. If, on the other hand, we use the same combination of symbols for one thing one day and for another the next, we abuse our symbols instead of using them, and those who indulge in slovenly habits in this respect ere long lose the power alike of thinking and of expressing themselves correctly. The symbols, however, in the first instance, may be anything in the wide world that we have a fancy for. They have no more to do with the ideas they serve to convey than money has with the things that it serves to buy.

The principle of association, as everyone knows, involves that whenever two things have been associated sufficiently together, the suggestion of one of them to the mind shall immediately raise a suggestion of the other. It is in virtue of this principle that language, as we call it, exists at all, for the essence of language consists, as I have said perhaps already too often, in the fixity with which certain ideas are invariably connected with certain symbols. But this being so, it is hard to see how we can deny that the lower animals possess the germs of a highly rude and unspecialized, but still true language, unless we also deny that they have any ideas at all; and this I gather is what Professor Max Müller in a quiet way rather wishes to do. Thus he says, "It is easy enough to show that animals communicate, but this is a fact which has never been doubted. Dogs who growl and bark leave no doubt in the minds of other dogs or cats, or even of man, of what they mean, but growling and barking are not language, nor do they even contain the elements of language." [2]

I observe the Professor says that animals communicate without saying what it is that they communicate. I believe this to have been because if he said that the lower animals communicate their ideas, this would be to admit that they have ideas; if so, and if, as they present every appearance of doing, they can remember, reflect upon, modify these ideas according to modified surroundings, and inter-

[2] Max Müller, *Three Lectures on the Science of Language* (New York: Longmans, Green & Co., Inc., 1889), p. 4.

change them with one another, how is it possible to deny them the germs of thought, language, and reason—not to say a good deal more than the germs? It seems to me that not knowing what else to say that animals communicated if it was not ideas, and not knowing what mess he might not get into if he admitted that they had ideas at all, he thought it safer to omit his accusative case altogether.

That growling and barking cannot be called a very highly specialized language goes without saying; they are, however, so much diversified in character, according to circumstances, that they place a considerable number of symbols at an animal's command, and he invariably attaches the same symbol to the same idea. A cat never purrs when she is angry, nor spits when she is pleased. When she rubs her head against anyone affectionately it is her symbol for saying that she is very fond of him, and she expects, and usually finds that it will be understood. If she sees her mistress raise her hand as though to pretend to strike her, she knows that it is the symbol her mistress invariably attaches to the idea of sending her away, and as such she accepts it. Granted that the symbols in use among the lower animals are fewer and less highly differentiated than in the case of any known human language, and therefore that animal language is incomparably less subtle and less capable of expressing delicate shades of meaning than our own, these differences are nevertheless only those that exist between highly developed and inchoate language; they do not involve those that distinguish language from no language. They are the differences between the undifferentiated protoplasm of the amoeba and our own complex organization; they are not the differences between life and no life. In animal language as much as in human there is a mind intentionally making use of a symbol accepted by another mind as invariably attached to a certain idea, in order to produce that idea in the mind which it is desired to affect—more briefly, there is a sayer, a sayee, and a covenanted symbol designedly applied. Our own speech is vertebrated and articulated by means of nouns, verbs, and the rules of grammar. A dog's speech is invertebrate, but I do not see how it is possible to deny that it possesses all the essential elements of language.

I have said nothing about Professor R. L. Garner's researches into the language of apes, because they have not yet been so far verified and accepted as to make it safe to rely upon them; but when he lays it down that all voluntary sounds are the products of thought, and that, if they convey a meaning to another, they perform the functions of human speech, he says what I believe will commend itself to any unsophisticated mind. I could have wished, however, that he had not limited himself to sounds, and should have preferred his saying what I doubt not he would readily accept—I mean, that all symbols or tokens of whatever kind, if voluntarily adopted as such, are the products of thought, and perform the functions of human speech; but I cannot too often remind you that nothing can be considered as fulfilling the conditions of language, except a voluntary application of a recognized token in order to convey a more or less definite meaning, with the intention doubtless of thus purchasing as it were some other desired meaning and consequent sensation. It is astonishing how closely in this respect money and words resemble one another. Money indeed may be considered as the most universal and expressive of all languages. For gold and silver coins are no more money when not in the actual process of being voluntarily used in purchase, than words not so in use are language. Pounds, shillings, and pence are recognized covenanted tokens, the outward and visible signs of an inward and spiritual purchasing power, but till in actual use they are only potential money, as the symbols of language, whatever they may be, are only potential language till they are passing between two minds. It is the power and will to apply the symbols that alone gives life to money, and as long as these are in abeyance the money is in abeyance also; the coins may be safe in one's pocket, but they are as dead as a log till they begin to burn in it, and so are our words till they begin to burn within us.

The real question, however, as to the substantial underlying identity between the language of the lower animals and our own, turns upon that other question whether or no, in spite of an immeasurable difference of degree, the thought and reason of man and of the lower animals is essentially the same. No one will expect a dog to master and express the varied ideas that are incessantly arising in connection with human affairs. He is a pauper as against a millionaire. To ask him to do so would be like giving a street-boy sixpence and telling him to go and buy himself a founder's share in the New River Company. He would not even know what was meant, and even if he did it would take several millions of sixpences to buy one. It is astonishing what a clever workman will do with very modest tools, or again how far a thrifty housewife will make a very small sum of money go, or again in like manner how many ideas an intelligent brute can receive and convey with its very limited vocabulary; but no one will pretend that a dog's intelligence can ever reach the level of a man's. What we do maintain is that, within its own limited range, it is of the same essential character as our own, and that though a dog's ideas in respect of human affairs are both vague and narrow, yet in respect of canine affairs they are precise enough and extensive enough to deserve no other name than thought or reason. We hold moreover that they communicate their ideas in essentially the same manner as we do—that is to say, by the instrumentality of a code of symbols attached to certain states of mind and material objects, in the first instance arbitrarily, but so persistently, that the presentation of the symbol immediately carries with it the idea which it is intended to convey. Animals can thus receive and impart ideas on all that most concerns them. As my great namesake said some two hundred years ago, they know "what's what, and that's as high as metaphysic can fly." And they not only know what's what themselves, but can impart to one another any new what's-whatness that they may have acquired, for they are notoriously able to instruct and correct one another.

Against this Professor Max Müller contends that we can know nothing of what goes on in the mind of any lower animal, inasmuch as we are not lower animals ourselves. "We can imagine anything we like about what passes in the mind of an animal," he writes, "we can know absolutely nothing." [3] It is something to have it in evidence that he conceives animals as having a mind at all, but it is not easy to see how they can be supposed to have a mind, without being able to acquire ideas, and having acquired, to read, mark, learn, and inwardly digest them. Surely the mistake of requiring too much evidence is hardly less great than that of being contended with too little. We, too, are animals, and can no more refuse to infer reason from certain visible actions in their case than we can in our own. If Professor Max Müller's plea were allowed, we should have to deny our right to infer confidently what passes in the mind of anyone not ourselves, inasmuch as we are not that person. We never, indeed, can obtain irrefragable certainty about this or any other matter, but we can be sure enough in many cases to warrant our staking all that is most precious to us on the soundness of our opinion. Moreover, if the Professor denies our right to infer that animals reason, on the ground that we are not animals enough ourselves to be able to form an opinion, with what right does he infer so confidently himself that they do not reason? And how, if they present every one of those appearances which we are accustomed to connect with the communication of an idea from one mind to another, can we deny that they have a language of their own, though it is one which in most

[3] Max Müller, *Science of Thought* (New York: Longmans, Green & Co., Inc., 1887), p. 9.

cases we can neither speak nor understand? How can we say that a sentinel rook, when it sees a man with a gun and warns the other rooks by a concerted note which they all show that they understand by immediately taking flight, should not be credited both with reason and the germs of language?

After all, a professor, whether of philology, psychology, biology, or any other ology, is hardly the kind of person to whom we should appeal on such an elementary question as that of animal intelligence and language. We might as well ask a botanist to tell us whether grass grows, or a meteorologist to tell us if it has left off raining. If it is necessary to appeal to anyone, I should prefer the opinion of an intelligent gamekeeper to that of any professor, however learned. The keepers, again, at the Zoological Gardens, have exceptional opportunities for studying the minds of animals—modified, indeed, by captivity, but still minds of animals. Grooms, again, and dog-fanciers, are to the full as able to form an intelligent opinion on the reason and language of animals as any University Professor, and so are cat's-meat men. I have repeatedly asked gamekeepers and keepers at the Zoological Gardens whether animals could reason and converse with one another, and have always found myself regarded somewhat contemptuously for having even asked the question. I once said to a friend, in the hearing of a keeper at the Zoological Gardens, that the penguin was very stupid. The man was furious, and jumped upon me at once. "He's not stupid at all," said he; "he's very intelligent."

Who has not seen a cat, when it wishes to go out, raise its fore paws on to the handle of the door, or as near as it can get, and look round, evidently asking someone to turn it for her? It is reasonable to deny that a reasoning process is going on in the cat's mind, whereby she connects her wish with the steps necessary for its fulfilment, and also with certain invariable symbols which she knows her master or mistress will interpret? Once, in company with a friend, I watched a cat playing with a house-fly in the window of a ground-floor room. We were in the street, while the cat was inside. When we came up to the window she gave us one searching look, and, having satisfied herself that we had nothing for her, went on with her game. She knew all about the glass in the window, and was sure we could do nothing to molest her, so she treated us with absolute contempt, never even looking at us again.

The game was this. She was to catch the fly and roll it round and round under her paw along the window sill, but so gently as not to injure it nor prevent it from being able to fly again when she had done rolling it. It was very early spring, and flies were scarce, in fact there was not another in the whole window. She knew that if she crippled this one, it would not be able to amuse her further, and that she would not readily get another instead, and she liked the feel of it under her paw. It was soft and living, and the quivering of its wings tickled the ball of her foot in a manner that she found particularly grateful; so she rolled it gently along the whole length of the window sill. It then became the fly's turn. He was to get up and fly about in the window, so as to recover himself a little; then she was to catch him again, and roll him softly all along the window sill, as she had done before.

It was plain that the cat knew the rules of her game perfectly well, and enjoyed it keenly. It was equally plain that the fly could not make head or tail of what it was all about. If it had been able to do so it would have gone to play in the upper part of the window, where the cat could not reach it. Perhaps it was always hoping to get through the glass, and escape that way; anyhow, it kept pretty much to the same pane, no matter how often it was rolled. At last, however, the fly, for some reason or another, did not reappear on the pane, and the cat began looking everywhere to find it. Her annoyance when she failed to do so was extreme. It was not only that she had lost her fly, but that she could not conceive how she should have ever come to do so. Presently she noted a small knot in the woodwork of the sill, and it flashed upon her that she had accidentally killed the fly, and that this was its dead body. She tried to move it gently with her paw, but it was no use, and for the time she satisfied herself that the knot and the fly had nothing to do with one another. Every now and then, however, she returned to it as though it were the only thing she could think of, and she would try it again. She seemed to say she was certain there had been no knot there before—she must have seen it if there had been; and yet, the fly could hardly have got jammed so firmly into the wood. She was puzzled and irritated beyond measure, and kept looking in the same place again and again, just as we do when we have mislaid something. She was rapidly losing temper and dignity when suddenly we saw the fly reappear from under the cat's stomach and make for the windowpane, at the very moment when the cat herself was exclaiming for the fiftieth time that she wondered where that stupid fly ever could have got to. No man who has been hunting twenty minutes for his spectacles could be more delighted when he suddenly finds them on his own forehead. "So that's where you were," we seemed to hear her say, as she proceeded to catch it, and again began rolling it very softly without hurting it, under her paw.

My friend and I both noticed that the cat, in spite of her perplexity, never so much as hinted that we were the culprits. The question whether anything outside the window could do her good or harm had long since been settled by her in the negative, and she was not going to reopen it; she simply cut us dead, and though her annoyance was so great that she was manifestly ready to lay the blame on anybody or anything with or without reason, and though she must have perfectly well known that we were watching the whole affair with amusement, she never either asked us if we had happened to see such a thing as a fly go down our way lately, or accused us of having taken it from her—both of which ideas she would, I am confident, have been very well able to convey to us if she had been so minded.

Now what are thought and reason if the processes that were going through this cat's mind were not both one and the other? It would be childish to suppose that the cat thought in words of its own, or in anything like words. Its thinking was probably conducted through the instrumentality of a series of mental images. We so habitually think in words ourselves that we find it difficult to realize thought without words at all; our difficulty, however, in imagining the particular manner in which the cat thinks has nothing to do with the matter. We must answer the question whether she thinks or no, not according to our own ease or difficulty in understanding the particular manner of her thinking, but according as her action does or does not appear to be of the same character as other action that we commonly call thoughtful. To say that the cat is not intelligent, merely on the ground that we cannot ourselves fathom her intelligence—this, as I have elsewhere said, is to make intelligence mean the power of being understood, rather than the power of understanding. This nevertheless is what, for all our boasted intelligence, we generally do. The more we can understand an animal's ways, the more intelligent we call it, and the less we can understand these, the more stupid do we declare it to be. As for plants—whose punctuality and attention to all the details and routine of their somewhat restricted lines of business is as obvious as it is beyond all praise—we understand the working of their minds so little that by common consent we declare them to have no intelligence at all.

Before concluding I should wish to deal a little more fully with Professor Max Müller's contention that there can be no reason without language, and no language without reason. Surely when two practised pugilists are fighting, parrying each other's blows, and

watching keenly for an unguarded point, they are thinking and reasoning very subtly the whole time, without doing so in words. The
machination of their thoughts, as well as its expression, is actual
—I mean, effectuated and expressed by action and deed, not words.
They are unaware of any logical sequence of thought that they could
follow in words as passing through their minds at all. They may
perhaps think consciously in words now and again, but such thought
will be intermittent, and the main part of the fighting will be done
without any internal concomitance of articulated phrases. Yet we
cannot doubt that their action, however much we may disapprove
of it, is guided by intelligence and reason; nor should we doubt that
a reasoning process of the same character goes on in the minds of
two dogs or fighting-cocks when they are striving to master their
opponents.

Do we think in words, again, when we wind up our watches, put
on our clothes, or eat our breakfasts? If we do, it is generally about
something else. We do these things almost as much without the help
of words as we wink or yawn, or perform any of those other actions
that we call reflex, as it would almost seem because they are done
without reflection. They are not, however, the less reasonable because wordless.

Even when we think we are thinking in words, we do so only in
half measure. A running accompaniment of words no doubt frequently attends our thoughts; but, unless we are writing or speaking, this accompaniment is of the vaguest and most fitful kind, as we
often find out when we try to write down or say what we are thinking about, though we have a fairly definite notion of it, or fancy
that we have one, all the time. The thought is not steadily and
coherently governed by and molded in words, nor does it steadily
govern them. Words and thought interact upon and help one another, as any other mechanical appliances interact on and help the
invention that first hit upon them; but reason or thought, for the
most part, flies along over the heads of words, working its own
mysterious way in paths that are beyond our ken, though whether
some of our departmental personalities are as unconscious of what
is passing, as that central government is which we alone dub with
the name of "we" or "us," is a point on which I will not now touch.

I cannot think, then, that Professor Max Müller's contention that
thought and language are identical—and he has repeatedly affirmed
this—will ever be generally accepted. Thought is no more identical
with language than feeling is identical with the nervous system.
True, we can no more feel without a nervous system than we can

discern certain minute organisms without a microscope. Destroy the nervous system, and we destroy feeling. Destroy the microscope, and we can no longer see the animalcules; but our sight of the animalcules is not the microscope, though it is effectuated by means of the microscope, and our feeling is not the nervous system, though the nervous system is the instrument that enables us to feel.

The nervous system is a device which living beings have gradually perfected—I believe I may say quite truly—through the will and power which they have derived from a fountainhead, the existence of which we can infer, but which we can never apprehend. By the help of this device, and in proportion as they have perfected it, living beings feel ever with great definiteness, and hence formulate their feelings in thought with more and more precision. The higher evolution of thought has reacted on the nervous system, and the consequent higher evolution of the nervous system has again reacted upon thought. These things are as power and desire, or supply and demand, each one of which is continually outstripping, and being in turn outstripped by the other; but, in spite of their close connection and interaction, power is not desire, nor demand supply. Language is a device evolved sometimes by leaps and bounds, and sometimes exceedingly slowly, whereby we help ourselves alike to greater ease, precision, and complexity of thought, and also to more convenient interchange of thought among ourselves. Thought found rude expression, which gradually among other forms assumed that of words. These reacted upon thought, and thought again on them, but thought is no more identical with words than words are with the separate letters of which they are composed.

To sum up, then, and to conclude. I would ask you to see the connection between words and ideas as in the first instance arbitrary. No doubt in some cases an imitation of the cry of some bird or wild beast would suggest the name that should be attached to it; occasionally the sound of an operation such as grinding may have influenced the choice of the letters g, r, as the root of many words that denote a grinding, grating, grasping, crushing action; but I understand that the number of words due to direct imitation is comparatively few in number, and that they have been mainly coined as the result of connections so far-fetched and fanciful as to amount practically to no connection at all. Once chosen, however, they were adhered to for a considerable time among the dwellers in any given place, so as to become acknowledged as the vulgar tongue, and raise readily in the mind of the inhabitants of that place the ideas with which they had been artificially associated.

As regards our being able to think and reason without words, the Duke of Argyll has put the matter as soundly as I have yet seen it stated. "It seems to me," he wrote, "quite certain that we can and do constantly think of things without thinking of any sound or word as designating them. Language seems to me to be necessary for the progress of thought, but not at all for the mere act of thinking. It is a product of thought, an expression of it, a vehicle for the communication of it, and an embodiment which is essential to its growth and continuity; but it seems to me altogether erroneous to regard it as an inseparable part of cogitation."

The following passages, again, are quoted from Sir William Hamilton in Professor Max Müller's own book, with so much approval as to lead one to suppose that the differences between himself and his opponents are in reality less than he believes them to be.

"Language," says Sir W. Hamilton, "is the attribution of signs to our cognitions of things. But as a cognition must have already been there before it could receive a sign, consequently that knowledge which is denoted by the formation and application of a word must have preceded the symbol that denotes it. A sign, however, is necessary to give stability to our intellectual progress—to establish each step in our advance as a new starting-point for our advance to another beyond. A country may be overrun by an armed host, but it is only conquered by the establishment of fortresses. Words are the fortresses of thought. They enable us to realize our dominion over what we have already overrun in thought; to make every intellectual conquest the base of operations for others still beyond."

"This," says Professor Max Müller, "is a most happy illustration," and he proceeds to quote the following, also from Sir William Hamilton, which he declares to be even happier still.

"You have all heard," says Sir William Hamilton, "of the process of tunnelling through a sandbank. In this operation it is impossible to succeed unless every foot, nay, almost every inch of our progress be secured by an arch of masonry before we attempted the excavation of another. Now language is to the mind precisely what the arch is to the tunnel. The power of thinking and the power of excavation are not dependent on the words in the one case or on the mason-work in the other; but without these subsidiaries neither could be carried on beyond its rudimentary commencement. Though, therefore, we allow that every movement forward in language must be determined by an antecedent movement forward in thought, still, unless thought be accompanied at each point of its evolutions by a corresponding evolution of language, its further development is arrested."

Man has evolved an articulate language, whereas the lower animals seem to be without one. Man, therefore, has far outstripped them in reasoning faculty as well as in power of expression. This, however, does not bar the communications which the lower animals make to one another from possessing all the essential characteristics of language, and, as a matter of fact, wherever we can follow them we find such communications effectuated by the aid of arbitrary symbols covenanted upon by the living beings that wish to communicate, and persistently associated with certain corresponding feelings, states of mind, or material objects. Human language is nothing more than this in principle, however much further the principle has been carried in our own case than in that of the lower animals.

This being admitted, we should infer that the thought or reason on which the language of men and animals is alike founded differs as between men and brutes in degree but not in kind. More than this cannot be claimed on behalf of the lower animals, even by their most enthusiastic admirer.

Bluspels and
Flalansferes

by C. S. LEWIS

Philologists often tell us that our language is full of dead
metaphors. In this sentence, the word "dead" and the word "metaphors" may turn out to be ambiguous; but the fact, or group of
facts, referred to, is one about which there is no great disagreement.
We all know in a rough and ready way, and all admit, these things
which are being called "dead metaphors," and for the moment I
do not propose to debate the propriety of the name. But while their
existence is not disputed, their nature, and their relation to thought,
gives rise to a great deal of controversy. For the benefit of any who
happen to have avoided this controversy hitherto, I had better make
plain what it is, by a concrete example. Bréal in his *Semantics* often
spoke in metaphorical, that is consciously, rhetorically, metaphorical
language, of language itself. Messrs. Ogden and Richards in *The
Meaning of Meaning* took Bréal to task on the ground that "it is
impossible thus to handle a scientific subject in metaphorical terms."
Barfield in his *Poetic Diction* retorted that Ogden and Richards
were, as a matter of fact, just as metaphorical as Bréal. They had
forgotten, he complained, that all language has a figurative origin
and that the "scientific" terms on which they piqued themselves—
words like *organism, stimulus, reference*—were not miraculously
exempt. On the contrary, he maintained, "these authors who pro-
fessed to eschew figurative expressions were really confining themselves to one very old kind of figure; they were rigid under the spell
of those verbal ghosts of the physical sciences which today make up
practically the whole meaning-system of so many European minds." [1]
Whether Ogden and Richards will see fit, or have seen fit, to reply
to this, I do not know; but the lines on which any reply would run

[1] A. O. Barfield, *Poetic Diction*, 1928, pp. 139, 140. New ed. (London: Faber &
Faber, Ltd., 1952).

are already traditional. In fact the whole debate may be represented by a very simple dialogue.

A. You are being metaphorical.

B. You are just as metaphorical as I am, but you don't know it.

A. No, I'm not. Of course I know all about *attending* once having meant *stretching*, and the rest of it. But that is not what it means now. It may have been a metaphor to Adam—but I am not using it metaphorically. What I *mean* is a pure concept with no metaphor about it at all. The fact that it *was* a metaphor is no more relevant than the fact that my pen is made of wood. You are simply confusing derivation with meaning.

There is clearly a great deal to be said for both sides. On the one hand it seems odd to suppose that what we *mean* is conditioned by a dead metaphor of which we may be quite ignorant. On the other hand, we see from day to day, that when a man uses a current and admitted metaphor without knowing it, he usually gets led into nonsense; and when, we are tempted to ask, does a metaphor become so old that we can ignore it with impunity? It seems harsh to rule that a man must know the whole semantic history of every word he uses—a history usually undiscoverable—or else talk without thinking. And yet, on the other hand, an obstinate suspicion creeps in that we cannot entirely jump off our own shadows, and that we deceive ourselves if we suppose that a new and purely conceptual notion of *attention* has replaced and superseded the old metaphor of stretching. Here, then, is the problem which I want to consider. How far, if at all, is thinking limited by these dead metaphors? Is Anatole France in any sense right when he reduces "The soul possesses God" to "the breath sits on the bright sky"? Or is the other party right when it urges "Derivations are one thing. Meanings are another"? Or is the truth somewhere between them?

The first and easiest case to study is that in which we ourselves invent a new metaphor. This may happen in one of two ways. It may be that when we are trying to express clearly to ourselves or to others a conception which we have never perfectly understood, a new metaphor simply starts forth, under the pressure of composition or argument. When this happens, the result is often as surprising and illuminating to us as to our audience; and I am inclined to think that this is what happens with the great, new metaphors of the poets. And when it does happen, it is plain that our new understanding is bound up with the new metaphor. In fact, the situation is for our purpose indistinguishable from that which arises when we hear a new metaphor from others; and for that reason, it need not be separately discussed. One of the ways, then, in which we invent a new metaphor, is by *finding* it, as unexpectedly as we might find it in the pages of a book; and whatever is true of the new metaphors that we find in books will also be true of those which we reach by a kind of lucky chance, or inspiration. But, of course, there is another way in which we invent new metaphors. When we are trying to explain, to some one younger or less instructed than ourselves, a matter which is already perfectly clear in our own minds, we may deliberately, and even painfully, pitch about for the metaphor that is likely to help him. Now when this happens, it is quite plain that our thought, our power of meaning, is not much helped or hindered by the metaphor that we use. On the contrary, we are often acutely aware of the discrepancy between our meaning and our image. We know that our metaphor is in some respects misleading; and probably, if we have acquired the tutorial shuffle, we warn our audience that it is "not to be pressed." It is apparently possible, in this case at least, to use metaphor and yet to keep our thinking independent of it. But we must observe that it is possible, only because we have other methods of expressing the same idea. We have already our own way of expressing the thing: we could say it, or we suppose that we could say it, literally instead. This clear conception we owe to other sources—to our previous studies. We can adopt the new metaphor as a temporary tool which we dominate and by which we are not dominated ourselves, only because we have other tools in our box.

Let us now take the opposite situation—that in which it is we ourselves who are being instructed. I am no mathematician; and some one is trying to explain to me the theory that space is finite. Stated thus, the new doctrine is, to me, meaningless. But suppose he proceeds as follows.

"You," he may say, "can intuit only three dimensions; you therefore cannot conceive how space should be limited. But I think I can show you how that which must appear infinite in three dimensions, might nevertheless be finite in four. Look at it this way. Imagine a race of people who knew only two dimensions—like the Flatlanders. And suppose they were living on a globe. They would have no conception, of course, that the globe was curved—for it is curved round in that third dimension of which they have no inkling. They will therefore imagine that they are living on a plane; but they will soon find out that it is a plane which nowhere comes to an end; there are no edges to it. Nor would they be able even to

imagine an edge. For an edge would mean that, after a certain
point, there would be nothing to walk on; nothing below their
feet. But that *below* and *above* dimension is just what their minds
have not got; they have only backwards and forwards, and left
and right. They would thus be forced to assert that their globe,
which they could not see as a globe, was infinite. You can see perfectly well that it is finite. And now, can you not conceive that as
these Flatlanders are to you, so you might be to a creature that
intuited four dimensions? Can you not conceive how that which
seems necessarily infinite to your three-dimensional consciousness
might none the less be really finite?" The result of such a metaphor
on my mind would be—in fact, has been—that something which
before was sheerly meaningless acquires at least a faint hint of
meaning. And if the particular example does not appeal to every
one, yet every one has had experiences of the same sort. For all of
us there are things which we cannot fully understand at all, but of
which we can get a faint inkling by means of metaphor. And in
such cases the relation between the thought and the metaphor is
precisely the opposite of the relation which arises when it is we
ourselves who understand and then invent the metaphors to help
others. We are here entirely at the mercy of the metaphor. If our
instructor has chosen it badly, we shall be thinking nonsense. If we
have not got the imagery clearly before us, we shall be thinking
nonsense. If we have it before us without knowing that it is metaphor—if we forget that our Flatlanders on their globe are a copy of
the thing and mistake them for the thing itself—then again we
shall be thinking nonsense. What truth we can attain in such a
situation depends rigidly on three conditions. First, that the imagery should be originally well chosen; secondly, that we should
apprehend the exact imagery; and thirdly that we should know
that the metaphor is a metaphor. (That metaphors, misread as
statements of fact, are the source of monstrous errors, need hardly
be pointed out.)

I have now attempted to show two different kinds of metaphorical
situation as they are at their birth. They are the two extremes, and
furnish the limits within which our inquiry must work. On the
one hand, there is the metaphor which we invent to teach by; on
the other, the metaphor from which we learn. They might be called
the Master's metaphor, and the Pupil's metaphor. The first is freely
chosen; it is one among many possible modes of expression; it does
not at all hinder, and only very slightly helps, the thought of its
maker. The second is not chosen at all; it is the unique expression

of a meaning that we cannot have on any other terms; it dominates completely the thought of the recipient; his truth cannot rise above the truth of the original metaphor. And between the Master's metaphor and the Pupil's there comes, of course, an endless number of types, dotted about in every kind of intermediate position. Indeed, these Pupil-Teachers' metaphors are the ordinary stuff of our conversation. To divide them into a series of classes and sub-classes and to attempt to discuss these separately would be very laborious, and, I trust, unnecessary. If we can find a true doctrine about the two extremes, we shall not be at a loss to give an account of what falls between them. To find the truth about any given metaphorical situation will merely be to plot its position. In so far as it inclines to the "magistral" extreme, so far our thought will be independent of it; in so far as it has a "pupillary" element, so far it will be the unique expression, and therefore the iron limit of our thinking. To fill in this framework would be, as Aristotle used to say, "anybody's business."

Our problem, it will be remembered, was the problem of "dead" or "forgotten" metaphors. We have now gained some light on the relation between thought and metaphor as it is at the outset, when the metaphor is first made; and we have seen that this relation varies greatly according to what I have called the "metaphorical situation." There is, in fact, one relation in the case of the Master's metaphor, and an almost opposite relation in that of the Pupil's metaphor. The next step must clearly be to see what becomes of these two relations as the metaphors in question progress to the state of death or fossilization.

The question of the Master's Metaphor need not detain us long. I may attempt to explain the Kantian philosophy to a pupil by the following metaphor. "Kant answered the question 'How do I know that whatever comes round the corner will be blue?' by the supposition 'I am wearing blue spectacles.'" In time I may come to use "the blue spectacles" as a kind of shorthand for the whole Kantian machinery of the categories and forms of perception. And let us suppose, for the sake of analogy with the real history of language, that I continue to use this expression long after I have forgotten the metaphor which originally gave rise to it. And perhaps by this time the form of the word will have changed. Instead of the "blue spectacles" I may now talk of the *bloospel* or even the *bluspel*. If I live long enough to reach my dotage I may even enter on a philological period in which I attempt to find the derivation of this mysterious word. I may suppose that the second element is derived

from the word *spell* and look back with interest on the supposed
period when Kant appeared to me to be magical; or else, arguing
that the whole word is clearly formed on the analogy of *gospel*,
may indulge in unhistorical reminiscenses of the days when the
Critique seemed to me irrefragably true. But how far, if at all, will
my thinking about Kant be affected by all this linguistic process? In
practice, no doubt, there will be some subtle influence; the mere
continued use of the word *bluspel* may have led me to attribute
to it a unity and substantiality which I should have hesitated to
attribute to "the whole Kantian machinery of the categories and
forms of perception." But that is a result rather of the noun-making
than of the death of the metaphor. It is an interesting fact, but
hardly relevant to our present inquiry. For the rest, the mere for-
getting of the metaphor does not seem to alter my thinking about
Kant, just as the original metaphor did not limit my thinking
about Kant; provided always—and this is of the last importance—
that it was, to begin with, a genuine Master's metaphor. I had my
conception of Kant's philosophy before I ever thought of the blue
spectacles. If I have continued philosophical studies I have it still.
The "blue spectacles" phrase was from the first a temporary dress
assumed by my thought for a special purpose, and ready to be laid
aside at my pleasure; it did not penetrate the thinking itself, and its
subsequent history is irrelevant. To any one who attempts to refute
my later views on Kant by telling me that I don't know the real
meaning of *bluspel,* I may confidently retort "Derivations aren't
meanings." To be sure, if there was any *pupillary* element in its
original use, if I received, as well as gave, new understanding when
I used it, then the whole situation will be different. And it is fair
to admit that in practice very few metaphors can be purely magistral; only that which to some degree enlightens ourselves is likely to
enlighten others. It is hardly possible that when I first used the metaphor of the blue spectacles I did not gain some new awareness of
the Kantian philosophy; and, so far, it was not purely magistral. But
I am deliberately idealizing for the sake of clarity. Purely magistral
metaphor may never occur. What is important for us is to grasp that
just in so far as any metaphor began by being magistral, so far I can
continue to use it long after I have forgotten its metaphorical
nature, and my thinking will be neither helped nor hindered by
the fact that it was originally a metaphor, nor yet by my forgetful-
ness of that fact. It is a mere accident. Here, derivations are irrelevant to meanings.

Let us now turn to the opposite situation, that of the Pupil's

Metaphor. And let us continue to use our old example of the un-mathematical man who has had the finitude of space suggested to him (we can hardly say "explained") by the metaphor of the Flat-landers on their sphere. The question here is rather more compli-cated. In the case of the Master's metaphor, by hypothesis, the master knew, and would continue to know, what he meant, inde-pendently of the metaphor. In the present instance, however, the fossilization of the metaphor may take place in two different ways. The pupil may himself become a mathematician, or he may remain as ignorant of mathematics as he was before; and in either case, he may continue to use the metaphor of the Flatlanders while for-getting its real content and its metaphorical nature.

I will take the second possibility first. From the imagery of the Flatlanders' sphere I have got my first inkling of the new meaning. My thought is entirely conditioned by this imagery. I do not ap-prehend the thing at all, except by seeing "it could be something like this." Let us suppose that in my anxiety to docket this new experience, I label the inkling or vague notion, "the Flatlanders' sphere." When I next hear the fourth dimension spoken of, I shall say, "Ah yes—the Flatlanders' sphere and all that." In a few years (to continue our artificial parallel) I may be talking glibly of the *Flalansfere* and may even have forgotten the whole of the im-agery which this word once represented. And I am still, according to the hypothesis, profoundly ignorant of mathematics. My situation will then surely be most ridiculous. The meaning of *Flalansfere* I never knew except through the imagery. I could get beyond the imagery, to that whereof the imagery was a copy, only by learning mathematics; but this I have neglected to do. Yet I have lost the imagery. Nothing remains, then, but the conclusion that the word *Flalansfere* is now really meaningless. My thinking, which could never get beyond the imagery, at once its boundary and its support, has now lost that support. I mean strictly nothing when I speak of the *Flalansfere*. I am only talking, not thinking, when I use the word. But this fact will be long concealed from me, because *Flalansfere,* being a noun, can be endlessly fitted into various con-texts, so as to conform to syntactical usage and to give an appearance of meaning. It will even conform to the logical rules; and I can make many judgments about the *Flalansfere;* such as *it is what it is,* and has *attributes* (for otherwise of course it wouldn't be a thing, and if it wasn't a thing, how could I be talking about it?), and is a *substance* (for it can be the subject of a sentence). And what *affec-tive* overtones the word may have taken on by that time, it is dangerous to predict. It had an air of mystery from the first: before the end I shall probably be building temples to it, and exhorting my countrymen to fight and die for the *Flalansfere*. But the *Flalansfere*, when once we have forgotten the metaphor, is only a noise.

But how if I proceed, after once having grasped the metaphor of the Flatlanders, to become a mathematician? In this case, too, I may well continue to use the metaphor, and may corrupt it in form till it becomes a single noun, the *Flalansfere*. But I shall have advanced, by other means, from the original symbolism; and I shall be able to study the thing symbolized without reference to the metaphor that first introduced me to it. It will then be no harm though I should forget that *Flalansfere* had ever been metaphorical. As the metaphor, even if it survived, would no longer limit my thoughts, so its fossilization cannot confuse them.

The results which emerge may now be summarized as follows. Our thought is independent of the metaphors we employ, in so far as these metaphors are optional: that is, in so far as we are able to have the same idea without them. For that is the real characteristic both of the magistral metaphors and of those which become optional, as the Flatlanders would become, if the pupil learned mathematics. On the other hand, where the metaphor is our only method of reaching a given idea at all, there our thinking is limited by the metaphor so long as we retain the metaphor; and when the metaphor becomes fossilized, our "thinking" is not thinking at all, but mere sound or mere incipient movements in the larynx. We are now in a position to reply to the statement that "Derivations are not meanings," and to the claim that "we know what we mean by words without knowing the fossilized metaphors they contain." We can see that such a statement, as it stands, is neither wholly true nor wholly false. The truth will vary from word to word, and from speaker to speaker. No rule of thumb is possible, we must take every case on its merits. A word can bear a meaning in the mouth of a speaker who has forgotten its hidden metaphor, and a meaning independent of that metaphor, but only on certain conditions. Either the metaphor must have been optional from the beginning, and have remained optional through all the generations of its use, so that the conception has always used and still uses the imagery as a mere tool; or else, at some period subsequent to its creation, we must have gone on to acquire, independently of the metaphor, such new knowledge of the object indicated by it as enables us now, at least, to dispense with it. To put the same thing in another way, meaning is independent of derivation, only if the

metaphor was originally "magistral"; or if, in the case of an originally pupillary metaphor, some quite new kind of apprehension has
arisen to replace the metaphorical apprehension which has been lost.
The two conditions may be best illustrated by a concrete example.
Let us take the word for *soul* as it exists in the Romance language.
How far is a man entitled to say that what he means by the word
âme or *anima* is quite independent of the image of *breathing,* and
that he means just the same (and just as much) whether he happens
to know that "derivation" or not? We can only answer that it depends on a variety of things. I will enumerate all the formal possibilities for the sake of clearness: one of them, of course, is too
grotesque to appear for any other purpose.

(1). The metaphor may originally have been magistral. Primitive
men, we are to suppose, were clearly aware, on the one hand, of
an entity called *soul;* and, on the other, of a process or object called
breath. And they used the second figuratively to suggest the first—
presumably when revealing their wisdom to primitive women and
primitive children. And we may suppose, further, that this magistral
relation to the metaphor has never been lost: that all generations,
from the probably arboreal to the man saying "Blast your soul" in
a pub this evening, have kept clearly before them these two separate
entities, and used the one metaphorically to denote the other, while
at the same time being well able to conceive the soul unmeta-
phorically, and using the metaphor merely as a color or trope which
adorned but did not influence their thought. Now if all this were
true, it would unquestionably follow that when a man says *anima*
his meaning is not affected by the old image of breath; and also,
it does not matter in the least whether he knows that the word once
suggested that image or not. But of course all this is not true.

(2). The metaphor may originally have been pupillary. So far
from being a voluntary ornament or paedagogic device, the ideas of
breath or *something like breath* may have been the only possible
inkling that our parents could gain of the soul. But if this was so,
how does the modern user of the word stand? Clearly, if he has
ceased to be aware of the metaphorical element in *anima,* without
replacing the metaphorical apprehension by some new knowledge
of the soul, borrowed from other sources, then he will mean nothing
by it; we must not, on that account, suppose that he will cease to
use it, or even to use it (as we say) intelligibly—i.e. to use it in
sentences constructed according to the laws of grammar, and to
insert these sentences into those conversational and literary contexts

where usage demands their insertion. If, on the other hand, he has some independent knowledge of the entity which our ancestors indicated by their metaphor of breath, then indeed he may mean something.

I take it that it is this last situation in which we commonly suppose ourselves to be. It doesn't matter, we would claim, what the majestic root GNA really stood for: we have learned a great deal about *knowing* since those days, and it is these more recent acquisitions that we use in our thinking. The first name for a thing may easily be determined by some inconsiderable accident. As we learn more, we mean more; the radical meaning of the old syllables does not bind us; what we have learned since has set us free. Assuredly, the accident which led the Romans to call all Hellenes *Graeci* did not continue to limit their power of apprehending Greece. And as long as we are dealing with sensible objects this view is hardly to be disputed. The difficulty begins with objects of thought. It may be stated as follows.

Our claim to independence of the metaphor is, as we have seen, a claim to know the object otherwise than through that metaphor. If we can throw the Flatlanders overboard and still think the fourth dimension, then, and not otherwise, we can forget what *Flalansfere* once meant and still think coherently. That was what happened, you will remember, to the man who went on and learned mathematics. He came to apprehend that of which the Flatlanders' sphere was only the image, and consequently was free to think beyond the metaphor and to forget the metaphor altogether. In our previous account of him, however, we carefully omitted to draw attention to one very remarkable fact: namely, that when he deserted metaphor for mathematics, he did not really pass from symbol to symbolized, but only from one set of symbols to another. The equations and what-nots are as unreal, as metaphorical, if you like, as the Flatlanders' sphere. The mathematical problem I need not pursue further; we see at once that it casts a disquieting light on our linguistic problem. We have hitherto been speaking as if we had two methods of thought open to us: the metaphorical, and the literal. We talked as if the creator of a magistral metaphor had it always in his power to think the same concept *literally* if he chose. We talked as if the present-day user of the word *anima* could prove his right to neglect that word's buried metaphor by turning round and giving us an account of the soul which was not metaphorical at all. That he has power to dispense with the particular metaphor of *breath,* is of course agreed. But we have not yet inquired what he can substitute for it. If we turn to those who are most anxious to tell us about the soul—I mean the psychologists—we shall find that the word *anima* has simply been replaced by complexes, repressions, censors, engrams, and the like. In other words the *breath* has been exchanged for *tyings-up, shovings-back, Roman magistrates,* and *scratchings.* If we inquire what has replaced the metaphorical *bright sky* of primitive theology, we shall only get a *perfect substance,* that is, a *completely made lying-under,* or—which is very much better, but equally metaphorical—a universal Father, or perhaps (in English) a *loaf-carver,* in Latin a *householder,* in Romance *a person older than.* The point need not be labored. It is abundantly clear that the freedom from a given metaphor which we admittedly enjoy in some cases is often only a freedom to choose between that metaphor and others.

Certain reassurances may, indeed, be held out. In the first place, our distinction between the different kinds of metaphorical situation can stand; though it is hardly so important as we had hoped. To have a choice of metaphors (as we have in some cases) is to know more than we know when we are the slaves of a unique metaphor. And, in the second place, all description or identification, all direction of our own thought or another's, is not so metaphorical as definition. If, when challenged on the word *anima,* we proceed to define, we shall only reshuffle the buried metaphors; but if we simply say (or think) "what I am," or "what is going on in here," we shall have at least something before us which we do not know by metaphor. We shall at least be no worse off than the arboreal psychologists. At the same time, this method will not really carry us far. "What's going on here" is really the content of *haec anima:* for *anima* we want "*The sort of thing* that is going on here," and once we are committed to *sorts* and *kinds* we are adrift among metaphors.

We have already said that when a man claims to think independently of the buried metaphor in one of his words, his claim may sometimes be allowed. But it was allowed only in so far as he could really supply the place of that buried metaphor with new and independent apprehension of his own. We now see that this new apprehension will usually turn out to be itself metaphorical; or else, what is very much worse, instead of new apprehension we shall have simply words—each word enshrining one more ignored metaphor. For if he does not know the history of *anima,* how should he know the history of the equally metaphorical words in which he defines it, if challenged? And if he does not know their history and therefore their metaphors, and if he cannot define *them* without yet further metaphors, what can his discourse be but an endless ringing of the changes on such *bluspels* and *Flalansferes* as seem to mean, indeed, but do not mean? In reality, the man has played us a very elementary trick. He claimed that he could think without metaphor, and in ignorance of the metaphors fossilized in his words. He made good the claim by pointing to the knowledge of his object which he possessed independently of the metaphor; and the proof of this knowledge was the definition or description which he could produce. We did not at first observe that where we were promised a freedom from metaphor we were given only a power of changing the metaphors in rapid succession. The things he speaks of he has never apprehended *literally*. Yet only such genuinely literal apprehension could enable him to forget the metaphors which he was actually using and yet to have a meaning. Either literalness, or else metaphor understood: one or other of these we must have; the third alternative is nonsense. But literalness we cannot have. The man who does not consciously use metaphors talks without meaning. We might even formulate a rule: the meaning in any given composition is in inverse ratio to the author's belief in his own literalness.

If a man has seen ships and the sea, he may abandon the metaphor of a *sea-stallion* and call a boat a boat. But suppose a man who has never seen the sea, or ships, yet who knows of them just as much as he can glean, say from the following list of *Kenningar*—sea-stallions, winged logs, wave riders, ocean trains. If he keeps all these together in his mind, and knows them for the metaphors they are, he will be able to think of ships, very imperfectly indeed, and under strict limits, but not wholly in vain. But if instead of this he pins his faith on the particular kenning, *ocean trains,* because that kenning, with its comfortable air of machinery, seems to him somehow more safely prosaic, less flighty and dangerous than its fellows, and if, contracting that to the form *oshtrans,* he proceeds to forget that it was a metaphor, then, while he talks grammatically, he has ceased to think of anything. It will not avail him to stamp his feet and swear that he is literal; to say "An *oshtran* is an *oshtran,* and there's an end. I mean what I mean. What I mean is what I say."

The remedy lies, indeed, in the opposite direction. When we pass beyond pointing to individual sensible objects, when we begin to think of causes, relations, of mental states or acts, we become incurably metaphorical. We apprehend none of these things except through metaphor: we know of the ships only what the *Kenningar* will tell us. Our only choice is to use the metaphors and thus **to** think something, though less than we could wish; or else to be driven by unrecognized metaphors and so think nothing at all. I myself would prefer to embrace the former choice, as far as my ignorance and laziness allow me.

To speak more plainly, he who would increase the meaning and decrease the meaningless verbiage in his own speech and writing, must do two things. He must become conscious of the fossilized metaphors in his words; and he must freely use new metaphors, which he creates for himself. The first depends upon knowledge, and therefore on leisure; the second on a certain degree of imaginative ability. The second is perhaps the more important of the two: we are never less the slaves of metaphor than when we are making metaphor, or hearing it new made. When we are thinking hard of the Flatlanders, and at the same time fully aware that they *are* a metaphor, we are in a situation almost infinitely superior to that of the man who talks of the *Flalansfere* and thinks that he is being literal and straightforward.

If our argument has been sound, it leads us to certain rather remarkable conclusions. In the first place it would seem that we must be content with a very modest quantity of thinking as the core of all our talking. I do not wish to exaggerate our poverty. Not all our words are equally metaphorical, not all our metaphors are equally forgotten. And even where the old metaphor is lost there is often a hope that we may still restore meaning by pointing to some sensible object, some sensation, or some concrete memory. But no man can or will confine his cognitive efforts to this narrow field. At the very humblest we must speak of things in the plural; we must point not only to isolated sensations, but to groups and classes of sensations; and the universal latent in every group and every plural inflection cannot be thought without metaphor. Thus far beyond the security of literal meaning all of us, we may be sure, are going to be driven by our daily needs; indeed, not to go thus far would be to abandon reason itself. In practice we all really intend to go much farther. Why should we not? We have in our hands the key of metaphor, and it would be pusillanimous to abandon its significant use, because we have come to realize that its meaningless use is necessarily prevalent. We must indeed learn to use it more cautiously; and one of the chief benefits to be derived from our inquiry is the new standard of criticism which we must henceforward apply both to our own apparent thought and to that of others. We shall find, too, that real meaning, judged by this standard, does not come always where we have learned to expect.

Flalansferes and *bluspels* will clearly be most prevalent in certain types of writers. The percentage of mere syntax masquerading as meaning may vary from something like 100 per cent in political writers, journalists, psychologists, and economists, to something like forty per cent in the writers of children's stories. Some scientists will fare better than others: the historian, the geographer, and sometimes the biologist will speak significantly more often than their colleagues; the mathematician, who seldom forgets that his symbols are symbolic, may often rise for short stretches to ninety per cent of meaning and ten of verbiage. The philosophers will differ as widely from one another as any of the other groups differ among themselves: for a good metaphysical library contains at once some of the most verbal, and some of the most significant literature in the world. Those who have prided themselves on being literal, and who have endeavored to speak plainly, with no mystical tomfoolery, about the highest abstractions, will be found to be among the least significant of writers: I doubt if we shall find more than a beggarly five per cent of meaning in the pages of some celebrated "tough minded" thinkers, and how the account of Kant or Spinoza stands, none knows but heaven. But open your Plato, and you will find yourself among the great creators of metaphor, and therefore among the masters of meaning. If we turn to Theology—or rather to the literature of religion—the result will be more surprising still; for unless our whole argument is wrong, we shall have to admit that a man who says *heaven* and thinks of the visible sky is pretty sure to mean more than a man who tells us that heaven is a state of mind. It may indeed be otherwise; the second man may be a mystic who is remembering and pointing to an actual and concrete experience of his own. But it is long, long odds. Bunyan and Dante stand where they did; the scale of Bishop Butler, and of better men than he, flies up and kicks the beam.

It will have escaped no one that in such a scale of writers the poets will take the highest place; and among the poets those who have at once the tenderest care for old words and the surest instinct for the creation of new metaphors. But it must not be supposed that I am in any sense putting forward the imagination as the organ of truth. We are not talking of truth, but of meaning: meaning which is the antecedent condition both of truth and falsehood, whose antithesis is not error but nonsense. I am a rationalist. For me, reason is the natural organ of truth; but imagination is the organ of meaning. Imagination, producing new metaphors or revivifying old, is not the cause of truth, but its condition. It is, I confess, undeniable that such a view indirectly implies a kind of truth or rightness in the imagination itself. I said at the outset that the truth we won by metaphor could not be greater than the truth of the metaphor itself; and we have seen since that all our truth, or all but a few fragments, is won by metaphor. And thence, I confess, it does follow that if our thinking is ever true, then the metaphors by which we think must have been good metaphors. It does follow that if those original equations, between good and light, or evil and dark, between breath and soul and all the others, were from the beginning arbitrary and fanciful—if there is not, in fact, a kind of psycho-physical parallelism (or more) in the universe—then all our thinking is nonsensical. But we cannot, without contradiction, believe it to be nonsensical. And so, admittedly, the view I have taken has metaphysical implications. But so has every view.

Poetic Diction and Legal Fiction

by OWEN BARFIELD

The house of poetry contains many mansions. These mansions are so diverse in their qualities and in their effect on the indweller and some of them are so distant from others that the inhabitants of one mansion have sometimes been heard to deny that another is part of the same building at all. For instance, Edgar Allan Poe said that there is no such thing as a long poem, and the difference between a long narrative poem and a short lyric is admittedly rather baffling, seeming almost to be one of kind. What I have to say here touches mainly lyric poetry, and will interest those who love to dwell with recurring delight on special felicities of expression more than those to whom poetry means taking their *Iliad* or their *Faerie Queene* a thousand lines at a time and enjoying the story. It is highly specialized. Think for a moment of poems as of pieces of fabric, large tapestries, or minute embroideries as the case may be. What I have to say does not concern the whole form of even one of the embroideries, but only the texture itself, the nature of the process at any given point, as the fabric comes into being, the movements which the shuttle or the needle must have made. It is still more specialized than this; for in examining the texture of poetry one of the most important elements (a mansion to itself) is rhythm, sound, music; and all this is of necessity excluded. I am fully aware that this involves the corollary that the kind of poetry I am talking about may also be written in prose; but that is a difficulty which is chronic to the subject. I wish, however, to treat of that element in poetry which is best called "meaning" pure and simple. Not the meaning of poetry, nor the meaning of any poem as a whole, but just meaning. If this sounds like an essay in microscopy, or if it be objected that what I am talking about is not poetic diction, but etymology or philosophy or even genetic psychology, I can only reply that whatever it ought to

51

be called, it is, to some people, extraordinarily interesting, and that if, in all good faith, I have given it a wrong address, it is still to me the roomiest, the most commodious, and the most exciting of all the mansions which I rightly or wrongly include in the plan and elevation of the great house.

The language of poetry has always been in a high degree *figurative;* it is always illustrating or expressing what it wishes to put before us by comparing that with something else. Sometimes the comparison is open and avowed, as when Shelley compares the sky-lark to a poet, to a high-born maiden, and to a rose embowered in its own green leaves; when Keats tells us that a summer's day is:

> like the passage of an angel's tear
> That falls through the clear ether silently.

or when Burns writes simply: "My love is like a red red rose." And then we call it a "simile." Sometimes it is concealed in the form of a bare statement, as when Shelley says of the west wind, not that it is *like,* but that it *is* "the breath of Autumn's being," calls upon it to "make him its lyre" and says of himself that *his* leaves are falling. This is known as "metaphor." Sometimes the element of comparison drops still farther out of sight. Instead of saying that A is like B or that A is B, the poet simply talks about B, without making any overt reference to A at all. You know, however, that he intends A all the time, or, better say that you know he intends *an* A; for you may not have a very clear idea of what A is and even if you have got an idea, somebody else may have a different one. This is generally called "symbolism."

I do not say that these particular methods of expressions are an absolute *sine qua non* of poetic diction. They are not. Poetry may also take the form of simple and literal statement. But figurative expression is found everywhere; its roots descend very deep, as we shall see, into the nature, not only of poetry, but of language itself. If you took away from the stream of European poetry every passage of a metaphorical nature, you would reduce it to a very thin trickle indeed, pure though the remainder beverage might be to the taste. Perhaps our English poetry would suffer the heaviest damage of all. Aristotle, when treating of diction in his *poetics,* provides the right expression by calling the element of metaphor πολὺ μέγιστον—far the most important.

It may be noticed that I am now using the word "metaphor" in a slightly different and wider sense than when I placed it in the midst between simile on the one hand and symbol on the other. I am now using it, and shall use it frequently throughout this article, to cover the whole gamut of figurative language including simile and symbol. I do not think this need confuse us. Strict metaphor occurs about the middle of the gamut and expresses the essential nature of such language more perfectly perhaps than either of the extremes. In something the same way Goethe found that the leaf of a plant expressed its essential nature as plant, while the blossom and the root could be considered as metamorphoses of the leaf. Here I want to try and consider a little more closely what the essential nature of figurative language is and how that nature is most clearly apparent in the figure called metaphor.

But first of all let us return to the "gamut" and take some examples. This time let us move along it in the reverse direction, beginning from symbolism.

> Does the road wind uphill all the way?
>   Yes, to the very end.
> Will the day's journey take the whole long day?
>   From morn to night, my friend.
>
> But is there for the night a resting-place?
>   A roof for when the slow, dark hours begin.
> May not the darkness hide it from my face?
>   You cannot miss that inn.
>
> Shall I meet other wayfarers at night?
>   Those who have gone before.
> Then must I knock or call when just in sight?
>   They will not keep you waiting at that door.
>
> Shall I find comfort, travel-sore and weak?
>   Of labour you shall find the sum.
> Will there be beds for me and all who seek?
>   Yea, beds for all who come.

As I have already suggested, the ordinary way of characterizing this kind of language would be to say that the poet says one thing and means another. Is this true? Is it fair to say that Christina Rossetti says B but that she *really means* A? I do not think this is a question which can be answered with a simple "yes" or "no." In fact the difficult and elusive relation between A and B is the heart of my matter. For the time being let me hazard, as a rather hedging

sort of answer, that the truer it is to say "yes," the worse is the poem,
the truer it is to say "no," the better is the poem. We feel that B,
which is actually said, ought to be necessary, even inevitable in
some way. It ought to be in some sense the best, if not the only way,
of expressing A satisfactorily. The mind should dwell on it as well as
on A and thus the two should be somehow inevitably fused together
into one simple meaning. But if A is too obvious and could be
equally or almost as well expressed by other and more direct means,
then the mind jumps straight to A, remains focused on it, and loses
interest in B, which shrinks to a kind of dry and hollow husk. I
think this is a fault of Christina Rossetti's poem. We know just
what A is. A = "The good life is an effort" plus "All men are
mortal." Consequently it detaches itself from B, like a soul leaving
a body, and the road and the inn and the beds are not a real road
and inn and beds, they look faintly heraldic—or as if portrayed in
lacquer. They are not even poetically real. We never get a fair
chance to accord to their existence that willing suspension of disbelief which we are told constitutes "poetic faith."

I must here remark that merely making A obscure is not in itself
a recipe for writing good symbolical poetry. William Blake at his
worst, and, I fancy, many modern poets who write or intend to
write symbolically, go astray here. They are so anxious to avoid
the error of intending too obvious an A, so anxious to avoid a mere
old-fashioned simile, that we end by being mystified or disgusted
by the impossibility of getting any sort of feeling at all of what they
are talking about, or why. Why are they talking about B at all,
we ask ourselves. If they are doing it simply for the sake of B, it is
pure drivel. On the other hand, if they intend an A, what evidence
is there of it? We do not mind A being intangible, because it is still
only half born from the poet's unconscious, but you cannot make
poetry by cunningly removing all the clues which, if left, would
discover the staleness of your meaning. In other words, if you set
out to say one thing and mean another, you must really mean another, and that other must be worth meaning.

It will be observed that when we started from the simile and
moved towards the symbol, the criterion or yardstick by which we
measured our progress was the element of *comparison*—paramount
in the simile and very nearly vanished out of sight in the symbol.
When, on the other hand, we move backwards, starting from the
symbol, we find ourselves with another yardstick, viz. the fact of
saying one thing and meaning another. The poet says B but he
means A. He hides A in B. B is the normal everyday meaning which

the words so to speak "ought" to have on the face of them, and A
is what the poet *really* has to say to us, and which he can only say
through or alongside of, or by modifying, these normal everyday
meanings. A is his own new, original, or poetic meaning. If I were
writing this article in Greek or German, my public would no doubt
be severely restricted, but there would be this advantage to me—
that I could run the six words "say-one-thing-and-mean-another" together and use the resulting conglomerate as a noun throughout the
rest of it. I cannot do this, but I will make bold to borrow another
German word instead. The word *Tarnung* was, I believe, extensively
used under the heel of the Nazi tyranny in Germany for the pre-
cautionary practice of hiding one meaning in another, the allusion
being to the *Tarnhelm* of the Nibelungs. I shall give it an English
form and call it "Tarning." When I say "Tarning," therefore, the
reader is asked to substitute mentally the concept of saying one
thing and meaning another, in the sense in which I have just been
trying to expound it. We have already seen that the more A lives
as a modification or enrichment of B, the better is the tarning.

Now let us proceed to the next step in our backward progress from
symbol to simile. We come to the metaphor. And here we find both
the best and the most numerous examples of tarning. Almost any
poem, almost any passage of really vivid prose which you pick up
is sure to contain them in abundance. I will choose an example (the
source of which he does not disclose) given by Dr. Hugh Blair,
the eighteenth-century writer on style.

> Those persons who gain the hearts of most people, who are chosen
> as the companions of their softer hours, and their reliefs from anxiety
> and care, are seldom persons of shining qualities or strong virtues:
> it is rather *the soft green* of the soul on which we rest our eyes, that
> are fatigued with beholding more glaring objects.

Consider how the ordinary literal meaning of the word "green"
blends with the ineffable psychic quality which it is the writer's
object to convey! How much weaker it would be, had he written:
"It is rather persons whose souls we find restful, as the eye finds
green fields restful, &c." Put it that way and nearly all the tarning,
and with it half the poetry, is lost. The passage reminds me of this
from Andrew Marvell's *Garden*:

> The Mind, that Ocean where each kind
> Does straight its own resemblance find;

> Yet it creates, transcending these,
> Far other Worlds, and other Seas;
> Annihilating all that's made
> To a green Thought in a green Shade.

What a lot of tarning can be done with the word "green"!

We see that any striking and original use of even a single word tends to be metaphorical and shows us the process of tarning at work. On the whole, I think it is true to say that the fewer the words containing the metaphor, the more the expression is in the strict sense a "trope" rather than a metaphor—the more tarning we shall feel. For the long and elaborate metaphor is already almost a simile—a simile with the word "like" missed out. We must, however, remember that the tarning may not have actually occurred in the particular place where we find it. People copy one another and the metaphor may be a cliché or, if not a cliché, part of our common heritage of speech. Thus, when Tennyson writes:

> When the happy Yes
> Falters from her lips,
> Pass and blush the news
> Over glowing ships

we feel that the peculiarly effective use of the word "blush" throughout this lyric is a tarning of his own. It actually goes on in us as we read. When, on the other hand, Arnold writes in the *Scholar Gypsy:*

> O Life unlike to ours!
> Who fluctuate idly without term or scope

or:

> Vague half-believers of our casual creeds,
> Who never deeply felt, nor clearly willed,
> Whose insight never has borne fruit in deeds

though none of this writing can be described as cliché, yet we feel that the metaphorical element in "fluctuate" and in "borne fruit" is the product of a tarning that happened before Arnold was born. So, too, in the passage I first quoted the *"shining* qualities" and the *"softer* hours" are metaphors of the kind we are all using every day, almost without thinking of them as metaphors. We all speak of *clear* heads, of *brilliant* wit, of *seeing* somebody's meaning, of so and so being the *pick of the bunch,* and so on: and most of us must use at least, say, a hundred of these dead or half-dead metaphors every day of our lives. In fact, in dealing with metaphor, we soon find ourselves talking, not of poetry, but of language itself. Everywhere in language we seem to find that the process of tarning, or something very like it, either is or has been at work.

We seem to owe all these tropes and metaphors embedded in language to the fact that somebody at some time had the wit to say one thing and mean another, and that somebody else had the wit to tumble to the new meaning, to detect the bouquet of a new wine emanating from the old bottle. We owe them all to tarning, a process which we find prolifically at work wherever there is poetry— from the symbol, where it shouts at us and is all too easily mishandled, to the simile, where we already hear the first faint stirrings of its presence, inasmuch as the B image even here is modified, enriched, or colored by the A image with which it is this time overtly compared.

> Then fly our greetings, fly our speech and smiles!
> —As some grave Tyrian trader, from the sea,
>   Descried at sunrise an emerging prow
> Lifting the cool-hair'd creepers stealthily,
>   The fringes of a southward-facing brow
>   Among the Aegean isles;
> And saw the merry Grecian coaster come,
>   Freighted with amber grapes, and Chian wine,
>   Green bursting figs, and tunnies steep'd in brine;
> And knew the intruders on his ancient home,
>
> The young light-hearted masters of the waves.

The grave Tyrian trader and the merry Grecian coaster are not the same figures that we should meet in a history book. They have their own life, they take in the imagination a special color from the things with which they are compared—that is, the *Scholar Gypsy* on the one hand and our too modern selves on the other. They are pregnant with the whole of the poem that has gone before.

I said at the beginning that I might be accused of indulging in a kind of aesthetic microscopy. The drawback of the microscope is this, that even if the grain of sand which we see through it does indeed contain a world, mere magnification is not enough to enable us to see that world. Unfortunately the processes which are said to give to the infinitesimal a cosmic character are not merely minute;

they are also very rapid. This is certainly true of the process of tarning as it takes place in the mind of the poet and his reader. It is both rapid and delicate and, as the reader may have felt already, it is difficult to take it out and examine it without rushing in where angels fear to tread. But there is another modern invention which may be brought to the aid of the microscope in order to meet this drawback; and that is the slow-motion film. Can we find in any sphere of human life something analogous to a slow-motion picture of the tarning process? I think we can. I have said that tarning can be detected not only in accredited poetry or literature but also in the history of language as a whole. Is there any other human institution in which tarning also happens, and in which it happens on a broader scale and at a more leisurely pace? I think there is. I think we shall find such an illustration as we want in the law, notably in the development of law by means of fictions.

We are accustomed to find something crabbed and something comic in legal fictions. When we read in an old pleading an averment that the plaintiff resides in the Island of Minorca, "to wit in the parish of St. Mary le Bow in the Ward of Cheap"—or, in a Note in the *Annual Practice* for 1945, that every man-of-war is deemed to be situated permanently in the parish of Stepney—it sounds funny. But it must be admitted that it is not any funnier *per se* than Shelley's telling us that his leaves are falling or Campion informing us as to his mistress that "there is a garden in her face." It is funny when we take it literally, not particularly funny when we understand what is meant and why it is expressed in that particular way.

There is one kind of metaphor which occurs both in law and in poetry and which is on the whole commoner and less odd-sounding in modern law than it is in modern poetry. This is personification of abstractions:

> Let not Ambition mock their useful toil,
> Their homely joys, and destiny obscure;
> Nor Grandeur hear with a disdainful smile
> The short and simple annals of the poor.

We find this particular usage almost vanished from English poetry by the beginning of the twentieth century. The personification of abstractions and attributes which we find in the more high-flown sort of eighteenth-century poetry or in the occasional allegorical papers which Johnson inserted in the *Rambler* sound stiff

and unnatural to us, and a modern poet would hardly bring himself
to try and introduce the device at all. On the other hand, the
personification of limited companies by which they are enabled to
sue and be sued at law, to commit trespasses, and generally to be
spoken of as carrying on all sorts of activities which can only *really*
be carried on by sentient beings, is as common as dirt and no one
ever dreams of laughing at it. But these examples will hardly do for
our slow-motion picture. On the contrary, in them the gap between
the B meaning and the A meaning is as wide and the prima facie
absurdity of the B or surface-meaning is hardly less than in, let us
say, Ossian's description of the Hero: "In peace, thou art the Gale
of Spring, in war, the Mountain Storm."

The important thing is to see how and why the legal fiction comes
into being and what is its positive function in the life of human
beings. If you have suffered a wrong at the hands of another human
being, the practical question for you, the point at which law really
touches your life as a member of society, is, can you do anything
about it? Can you bring the transgressor to book and obtain resti-
tution? In other words, can you bring an action against him, obtain
judgment, and get that judgment executed? Now the answer to that
question must always depend to some extent, and in the earlier
stages of a society governed by law it depends to a very large extent
indeed on the answer to another question. It is not enough simply
to show that the transgressor has, in common parlance, broken the
law. What you or your advisers have to make up your mind about is
something rather different and often much more complicated. You
have to ask yourselves, Is there a form of procedure under which
I can move against him? If so, is it sufficiently cheap and expeditious
for me to be able to adopt it with some hope of success? Where, as
in the case of English Common Law down to the middle of the
nineteenth century, these forms of procedure, or forms of action
as they are more often called, are severely restricted in number, these
questions are very serious ones indeed.

While the so-called "historical" fictions (which are the only ones
I am concerned with) have no doubt played a broadly similar part
in every known system of law, I think it will be best if I confine
myself to England and take a particular example. The forms of
action were not the arbitrary inventions of an ingenious legislator.
They grew up out of the whole history of English social life, and
one of the results of this was a wide difference between those forms
of action which had their roots in the feudal system and those which
sprang from later and different sources. I think it is true to say that

they were different because they were really based on two different
ways of looking at human beings in society. You may look at a
human being in what I will call the genealogical way, in which
case you will conceive of his legal rights and position as being determined by what he *is* rather than by what he may choose to *do*.
They will then seem to be determined by the kind of father he had,
by the piece of land to which he and his ancestors were attached
or which was attached to them, and by its relations to adjoining
land attached to other people and their ancestors and descendants.
Or alternatively you may look at him in what I will call the personal
way, in which case his position will seem to be determined more by
the things which he himself has chosen to *do* of his own free will.
Maine in his *Ancient Law* calls the first way "Status" and the second
way "Contract," and he depicts society as evolving from the first
towards the second. Broadly speaking, forms of action having to do
with the ownership of land had grown up out of the first way, forms
of action having to do with the ownership of personal property out
of the second way, of looking at human beings.

Now suppose you had a good claim to the ownership of a piece
of land, perhaps with a pleasant house on it, which was in the possession of somebody else who also, but wrongfully, claimed to be
the owner. Your proper normal form of action, say, 500 years ago,
was by Writ of Right, a form of action which was very much of
the first type and hedged about accordingly with all sorts of ceremonies, difficulties, and delays.

At trahere atque moras tantis licet addere rebus!

One of the drawbacks of this type of action was that it was subject
to things called *Essoins*. Essoins seem to have corresponded roughly
to what we should call "adjournments"; they no doubt grew up
procedurally with a view to preventing an unscrupulous plaintiff
from taking unfair advantage of the defendant's ill health, absence,
or other accidental disability. But they must have been corn in
Egypt for a usurping defendant. I am tempted to let Ranulf de
Glanville (1130-1190),[1] in his own sedate language and at his own
pace, give the reader some idea of their nature and complexity:

If the Tenant, being summoned, appear not on the first day, but
Essoin himself, such Essoin shall, if reasonable, be received; and he

[1] John Beame's *Translation of Glanville* (London: A. H. & A. W. Reed Ltd.,
1812).

may, in this manner, essoin himself three times successively; and since the causes on account of which a person may justly essoin himself are various, let us consider the different kinds of Essoins.

Of Essoins, some arise on account of ill health, others from other sources.

(I will here interpose that, among the Essoins arising from other sources were the *de ultra mare* and the *de esse in peregrinatione* and that, if a person cast the Essoin *de esse in peregrinatione,* "it must be distinguished whether he went to Jerusalem or to another place. If to the former place, then a year and a day at least is generally allowed him." And with that I will let Glanville proceed again in his own order:)

Of those Essoins which arise from ill health, one kind is that *ex infirmitate veniendi,* another *ex infirmitate de reseantisa.*

If the Tenant, being summoned, should on the first day cast the Essoin *de infirmitate veniendi,* it is in the election of his Adversary, being present, either to require from the Essoiner a lawful proof of the truth of the Essoin in question on that very day, or that he should find pledges or bind himself solemnly that at the day appointed he will have his Warrantor of the Essoin . . . and he may thus Essoin himself three times successively. If on the third day, he neither appear nor essoin himself, then let it be ordered that he be forthcoming in person on another day; or that he send a fit Attorney in his place, to gain or lose for him . . . It may be asked, what will be the consequence if the Tenant appear at the fourth day, after having cast three Essoins, and warrant all the Essoins? In that case, he shall prove the truth of each Essoin by his own oath and that of another; and, on the same day, he shall answer to the suit. . . .

If anyone desire to cast the Essoin *de infirmitate de reseantisa,* he may thrice do it. Yet should the Essoiner, on the third day preceding that appointed, at a proper place and before a proper person, present his Essoin. If, on the third Summons the Tenant appear not, the Court should direct that it may be seen whether his indisposition amount to a languor, or not. For this purpose let the following Writ issue, directed to the Sheriff of the County . . . :

"The King to the Sheriff, Health. I command you that, without delay, you send 4 lawful men of your County to see if the infirmity of which B. hath essoined himself in my Court, against R., be a languor or not. And, if they perceive that it is a languor, then, that they should

put to him a day of one year and one day, from that day of the view,
to appear before me or my justices. . . ."

Nor was it forgotten that Essoiners themselves may be subject to
infirmities and languors:

> The principal Essoiner is also at liberty, if so disposed, to essoin
> himself by another Essoiner. In this case the second Essoiner must
> state to the Court that the Tenant, having a just cause of Essoin, had
> been detained, so that he could not appear at the day appointed,
> neither to lose nor gain, and that therefore he had appointed a certain
> other person to essoin him; and that the Essoiner himself had met with
> such an impediment, which had prevented his appearance on that day:
> and this he is prepared to prove according to the practice of the
> Court. . . .

Having at last succeeded in getting your opponent out of bed
and fixing the day for the trial, you still could not be certain that
he would not appear in Court followed (subject, no doubt, to Essoins)
by a professional boxer or swordsman, whom you would have to
tackle in lieu of calling evidence. And so on. And all this maybe
about a claim so clear that you could get it disposed of in five
minutes if you could only bring it to the stage of being tried at
all!

It would have been a very different matter, so perhaps your
Counsel would advise you, if only the issue were about *personal*
property instead of real property. We could go to a different Court
with a different form of action. No essoins. No wager of law. No
trial by battle. No trial by ordeal. Everything up to date and
efficient. What *is* personal property, you might ask. Well, your
horse for one thing and your hawk and your clothes and your
money—oh! yes, and oddly enough if you were a leaseholder instead
of a freeholder and had only a term of years in this precious piece
of land, *that* would be personal property too. But can't I get *my*
case heard by these people? Don't they understand anything about
fee simple? Oh! yes, they understand it all right; in fact they often
have to decide the point. For instance, if a leaseholder in possession
is ousted by a trespasser—by Jove! I've just thought of something!
And then if your Counsel had a touch of creative genius, he might
perhaps evolve the following device. It *was* evolved at all events, by
Tudor times or thereabouts and continued in use down to the
middle of the nineteenth century.

Remember the situation: You are the rightful owner of a piece of land of which X, who is in possession, wrongfully claims to be the owner. The device was this: you proceeded to inform the Court by your pleadings that you, as owner of the land, had recently leased it to a person whose name was John Doe, and John Doe had been ousted from his possession violently, *vi et armis,* by X, the Defendant. *You* were not bringing the action, you pretended: John Doe was; but as X might aver in his defence that the blameless Doe had no title, Doe has joined you, his landlord, in the proceedings to prove that you did have a good title at the time when you leased the land to him. By this means you got your case before the Court that had jurisdiction to deal with the action known as Ejectment, and were able to take advantage of the simpler and more effective procedure. Sometimes the fiction was a little more elaborate. Instead of alleging that X had ejected John Doe, you said that another gentleman called Richard Roe, or possibly William Stiles, had done so. Richard Roe having subsequently allowed X to take possession now claimed no interest in the proceedings, but he had given X notice that they were pending, so as to give X a chance to defend his title. In this case the first thing X heard of it all was a letter, signed "your loving friend, Richard Roe," telling him what had happened. Needless to say, John Doe and Richard Roe had no existence.

Many thousands of actions of this pattern and using these names must have been brought between the fifteenth and the nineteenth centuries and before long the whole procedure was no doubt so much a matter of course that it was little more than a kind of mathematical formula. There must, however, have been some earlier occasions on which it was a good deal more, and it is upon any one of these—perhaps the first of all—that I want the reader to bend his mind. Picture to yourself the Court, with Counsel on his feet opening the case. The story of John Doe and Richard Roe is being unfolded. At one point the Judge suddenly looks up and looks very hard at Counsel, who either winks very slightly or returns a stolid uncomprehending stare according to his temperament and the intimacy of his acquaintance with the Judge out of hours. But Counsel knows all the same what has happened. The Bench has tumbled to it. The Judge has guessed that there is no John Doe, no Richard Roe, no lease, no entry, no ouster. At the same moment, however, the Judge has seen the point of the whole fiction, the great advantage in the speedy administration of justice (for the real issue—the validity of X's title and yours—will be heard fairly and in full) and in

the extended jurisdiction of his own Court. He decides to accord
to the pleadings that willing suspension of disbelief which hundreds
of years later made Mr. Bumble say that the law was a "hass." The
case proceeds. Place this picture before your mind's eye and there
I think you will have a slow-motion picture of "tarning."

Has new law been made? It is much the same as asking whether
new language has been made when a metaphor disappears into a
"meaning." At all events, we begin to understand more fully what
Maitland meant, when he wrote of English law that "substantive
law has at first the look of being gradually secreted in the interstices
of procedure." This is particularly true of an unwritten system like
the English Common Law, where the law itself lay hidden in the
unconscious, until it was expressed in a judgment, and where rights
themselves depended on the existence of remedies. Consider that
very important fiction, which is very much alive and flourishing all
round us today—the fiction on which the law of trusteeship is based.
Anyone who is a trustee will know how absurdly remote from reality
is the B interpretation of his position, according to which he is the
"owner" of the trust property. Yet this fiction, which permeates the
whole of our jurisprudence, which most certainly is law, and not
merely procedure, was introduced in the first place by devices strictly
procedural, devices and circumstances which had their origin in
that same contrast between the genealogical and the personal conceptions of Society which gave us John Doe and Richard Roe.

Moreover, this fictitious ownership, which we call trusteeship,
has been strong enough to have other fictions erected on it. By the
Common Law the personal property of a married woman became
her husband's as soon as she married. But by a particularly ingenious
piece of tarning the equity judges expressed in the form of law,
and in doing so no doubt partly created, a more modern view of
the rights of married women. They followed the Common Law doctrine that the husband *owned* everything but, as to property which
someone had given to the wife with the intention that she should
have it for her own separate use, the Courts of Equity began in the
eighteenth century to say that the husband did indeed own this,
but he owned it as *trustee* for his wife; and they would prevent him
from dealing with it in any other way.

In the same way a metaphor may be strong enough to support a
metaphor, as when Shelley bids the west wind "Make me thy lyre
even as the forest is." If Shelley is not a lyre, neither is the forest;
yet he illustrates the one fiction with the other. Nor is there anything

grotesque or strained in this magnificent line. It is only when we begin to ponder and analyse it that we see how daring it is.

The long analogy which I have been drawing may be expressed more briefly in the formula:—metaphor: language: meaning:: legal fiction: law: social life. It has no particular significance if poetry is to be regarded *only* as either a pleasurable way of diverting our leisure hours or a convenient vehicle for the propagation of doctrine. For it must be conceded that there is all the difference in the world between the propagation of a doctrine and the creation of a meaning. The doctrine is already formulated and, if we choose to express it by tarning, that is simply a matter of technique or political strategy. The creation of meaning is a very different matter. I hope I may have succeeded in showing in the earlier part of this article that metaphor is something more than a piece of the technique of one of the fine arts. It is πολὺ μέγιστον not merely in the diction of poetry but in the nature and growth of language itself. So far we have only considered in this connection those ubiquitous figures of speech which are, or used to be, called "tropes," as when we speak of our lives *fluctuating*, of our insight *bearing fruit* in deeds, of *seeing the point*, and so on. But if we proceed to study language with a more definitely historical bias, and look into the etymologies and derivations of words, then the vast majority even of those meanings which we normally regard as "literal" are seen to have originated either in metaphors or in something like them. Such words as *spirit, sad, humor, perceive, attend, express, understand,* and so on immediately spring to the mind as examples. Indeed the difficulty here would rather be to find words that are *not* examples. There is no doubt that they were once metaphorical. The question which a good many people have asked themselves, a little uneasily, is, Are they *still* metaphors? And, if not, when—and still more *how*—precisely, did they cease to be so?

What is essential to the nature and growth of language is clearly essential to the nature and growth of our thought, or rather of our consciousness as a whole. In what way then is metaphor or tarning essential to that nature and that growth? Here we begin to tread on metaphysical ground and here I think the analogy of legal fictions can really help us by placing our feet on one or two firmer tufts in the quaking bog. It can help us to realize in firmer outlines certain concepts which, like all those relating to the nature of thought itself, are tenuous, elusive, and difficult of expression.

Students of history will have observed that rebellions and agitations arising out of dissatisfaction with the law tend, at any rate in the earlier stages of society, to demand, not so much a reform of the law as its *publication*. People complain that they do not know what the law is. They want to know what it is, because otherwise they cannot be sure that it will be the same tomorrow as it is today. In fact it is the very essence of a law that it should apply to every case. It follows that the forms of action must be limited in number, and they must not change from day to day. If there is a different law for every case that arises, then what is being administered is simply not law at all but the arbitrary (though not necessarily unjust) decisions of those who govern us. But that is exactly what the word law *means*—something which is *not* such a series of arbitrary decisions or events, something which will be *the same* for the next case as it was for the last. This is where the difficulty arises; for it is the nature of life itself (certainly of human life) never to repeat itself exactly. Phenomena exactly repeated are not life, they are mechanism. Life varies, law is of its nature unvarying. Yet at the same time it is the function of law to serve, to express, and indeed partly to *make* the social life of the community. That is the paradox, the diurnal solution of which constitutes the process called society. One solution is legislation, the other is fiction. Legislation is drastic, *a priori*, and necessary. Fiction is flexible, empirical, and also necessary. "Without the Fiction of Adoption," says Maine in his *Ancient Law*, "it is difficult to understand how Society would ever have escaped from its swaddling-clothes."

In the paradoxical relation of law to social life I think we have a useful picture of the paradoxical relation of language to consciousness. Formal logic is not much studied nowadays, but that does not alter the fact that logic is essential to the very existence of language and the forms of proposition and syllogism underlie all expression. Now logic presupposes first and foremost that the same word means the same thing in one sentence as it does in another. Humpty Dumpty may speak of making his words "mean" what he chooses, and if somebody made a noise never heard before or since he might possibly manage to convey some sort of vague sympathetic impression of the state of his feelings. Yet repetition is inherent in the very meaning of the word "meaning." To say a word "means" something implies that it means that same something more than once.

Here then is the paradox again. The logical use of language presupposes the meanings of the words it employs and presupposes them constant. I think it will be found to be a corollary of this, that the logical use of language can never add any meaning to it. The conclusion of a syllogism is implicit already in the premisses, that is, in the *meanings* of the *words* employed; and all the syllogism can do is to make that meaning clearer to us and remove any misconception or confusion. But life is not constant. Every man, certainly every original man, has something new to say, something new to mean. Yet if he wants to express that meaning (and it may be that it is only when he tries to express it, that he knows what he means) he must use language—a vehicle which presupposes that he must either mean what was meant before or talk nonsense!

If therefore he would say anything really new, if that which was hitherto unconscious is to become conscious, he must resort to tarning. He must talk what is nonsense on the face of it, but in such a way that the recipient may have the new meaning suggested to him. This is the true importance of metaphor. I imagine this is why Aristotle, in calling metaphor "the most important," gives as a reason that "it alone does not mean borrowing from someone else." In terms of mixed law and logic we might perhaps say that the metaphorical proposition contains a judgment, but a judgment pronounced with a wink at the Court. Bacon put it more clearly in the *Advancement of Learning* when he said:

> Those whose conceits are seated in popular opinions need only but to prove or dispute; but those whose conceits are beyond popular opinions have a double labour; the one *to make themselves conceived,* and the other to prove and demonstrate. So that it is of necessity with them to have recourse to similitudes and translations to express themselves.

If we consider Bacon's position in the history of thought, it will not surprise us that the problem should have presented itself to him so clearly. Himself a lawyer, was he not attempting to do for science the very thing which Maitland tells us those old legal fictions were contrived for, that is, "to get modern results out of medieval premisses"?

At all events there is a sentence in the *Novum Organum* which provides one of the most striking illustrations of tarning that it would be possible to imagine. It is a double illustration: first, there was an attempt at deliberate and fully conscious meaning-making, which failed: Bacon tried to inject new meaning into a word by *saying* precisely what he wanted it to mean. But we have seen that what is said precisely cannot convey new meaning. But, since his meaning *was* really new, there had at some point in the process to be a piece of actual tarning. There was—and it succeeded. He did in fact inject new meaning into another word—not by saying, but by just meaning it!

Licet enim in natura nihil vere existat praeter corpora individua edentia actus puros individuos ex lege; in doctrinis tamen, illa ipsa lex, ejusque inquisitio et inventio atque explicatio, pro fundamento est tam ad sciendum quam ad operandum. Eam autem legem ejusque paragraphos *formarum* nomine intelligimus; praesertim cum hoc vocabulum invaluerit, et familiariter occurrat.[2]

The "forms" of which Bacon here speaks were none other than the Platonic ideas, in which Bacon, of course, did not believe. What he did believe in was that system of abstract causes or uniformity which we have long since been accustomed to express by the phrase "the laws of nature," but for which there was then no name, because the meaning was a new one. He therefore tried deliberately by way of a *simile* to put this new meaning into the old word *"forma"*; but he failed, inasmuch as the new meaning never came into general use. Yet at the same time, more unconsciously, and by way of *metaphor,* he was putting the new meaning into the word *"lex"* itself— that curious meaning which it now bears in the expression "the laws of nature." This is one of those pregnant metaphors which pass into the language, so that much of our subsequent thinking is based on them. To realize that after all they *are* metaphors, and to ask what that entails, opens up avenues of inquiry which are beyond the province of this article. Certainly, they may be misleading, as well as illuminating. Long after Bacon's time, two great men—a lawyer who was concerned with the nature of law and a poet who was concerned with the nature of Nature—felt bound to draw attention to this very metaphor.

When an atheist [wrote Austin] speaks of *laws* governing the irrational world, the metaphorical application is suggested by an analogy still more slender and remote. . . . He means that the uniformity of succession and co-existence resembles the uniformity of

---

[2] Although it is true that in nature nothing exists beyond separate bodies producing separate motions according to law; still for the *study* of nature that very law and its investigation discovery and exposition are the essential thing, for the purpose both of science and of practice. Now it is that law and its clauses which we understand by the term "forms"—principally because this word is a familiar one and has become generally accepted. *Novum Organum,* ii. 2.

conduct produced by an imperative rule. If, to draw the analogy closer, he ascribes these laws to an author, he personifies a verbal abstraction and makes it play the legislator. He attributes the uniformity of succession and co-existence to *laws* set by *nature:* meaning by nature, the world itself; or perhaps that very uniformity which he imputes to nature's commands.[3]

The introduction of the atheist into this passage does not, I think, weaken its force as an illustration, for whatever the strength of Bacon's religious faith, it is quite plain that the "laws" of which he speaks in the *Novum Organum* have very little to do with the "commands" of any being other than nature itself.

> Long indeed, [says Coleridge in *The Friend*] will man strive to satisfy the inward querist with the phrase, laws of nature. But though the individual may rest content with the seeming metaphor, the race cannot. If a law of nature be a mere generalization, it is included . . . as an act of the mind. But if it be other and more, and yet manifestable only in and to an intelligent spirit, it must in act and substance be itself spiritual; for things utterly heterogeneous can have no intercommunion.

Perhaps we may supplement the last sentence by saying that an *apparent* intercommunion between things utterly heterogeneous is the true mark of metaphor and may be significant of spiritual substance. If this is so, and if the aptness of a metaphor to mislead varies inversely with the extent to which it continues to be felt and understood *as* a metaphor and is not taken in a confused way semiliterally, then the contemplation by the mind of legal fictions may really be a rather useful exercise. For these are devices of expression, of which the practical expediency can easily be understood, and whose metaphorical nature is not so easily forgotten as they pass into general use.

There is not much that is more important for human beings than their relations with each other, and it is these which laws are designed to express. The making and application of law are thus fundamental human activities, but what is more important for my purpose is that they bear the same relation to naked thinking as traveling does to map-reading or practice to theory. It is not by accident that such key words as *judgment* and *cause* have two distinct

[3] John Austin, *Lectures on Jurisprudence* (London: John Murray, Publishers, Ltd., 1869), I, 213.

meanings; the practical task of fixing personal responsibility must surely have been the soil from which, as the centuries passed, the abstract notion of cause and effect was laboriously raised. Accordingly it would be strange indeed if the study of jurisprudence were not well adapted to throw light on the mind and its workings.

That study was formerly regarded as an essential element in a liberal education. It was a distinguished Italian jurist, Giovanni Battista Vico, who at the turn of the seventeenth and eighteenth centuries became interested in the figurative element in language and evolved therefrom a theory of the evolution of human consciousness from an instinctive "poetic" wisdom (*sapienza poetica*) to the modern mode of analytical thought.

It is perhaps a pity that this respectful attitude to legal studies has long since been abandoned; a pity both on general grounds and because the vast change in man's idea of himself wrought by the new notions of evolution and development, and by the comparatively recent birth of historical imagination, have opened up rich new fields of speculation both in language and in law. A better and more widely diffused knowledge of the latter could hardly fail to be beneficial in far-reaching ways at a time when the whole theory of human society is in the melting-pot. For instance, a deeper, more sympathetic understanding of the long, slow movement of the human mind from the feudal, or genealogical, way of regarding human relationships towards what I have called the "personal" way would do no harm.

But I have been mainly concerned here with the subject of fictions. Properly understood, are they not a telling illustration of the fact that knowledge—the fullest possible awareness—of the nature of law is the true way of escape from its shackles? ἐγὼ γὰρ διὰ νόμου νόμῳ ἀπέθανον, "I, by the law, died unto the law," wrote St. Paul; and the *nature* of law, as law, is the same, whether it be moral, or logical, or municipal. If it be important for men to get a deep feeling for this process of liberation in general, it is equally important, for special reasons, that they should better comprehend the particular problem of the part played by metaphor in the operation and development of language. Here too the way to achieve liberation from the "confusion" of thought on which metaphor is based is not by attack or rebellion. The intrinsic nature of language makes all such attitudes puerile. It is not those who, like the optimistic Mr. Stuart Chase,[4] set out to cut away and expose all metaphorical usage who escape

---

[4] Stuart Chase, *The Tyranny of Words* (New York: Harcourt, Brace & World, Inc., 1938).

the curse of Babel. No. The best way to talk clearly and precisely and to talk sense is to understand as fully as possible the relation between predication and suggestion, between "saying" and "meaning." For then you will at least know what you are *trying* to do. It is not the freemen of a city who are likeliest to lose their way, and themselves, in its labyrinth of old and mazy streets; it is the simple-minded foreign nihilist making, with his honest-to-god intentions and suitcase, straight for the center, like a sensible man.

The Language of Magic

by BRONISLAW MALINOWSKI

The following general considerations on the nature of magical language in its relation to pragmatic speech do not, of course, claim the same degree of ripeness and finality as some of the more limited conclusions established on an exhaustive analysis of our own ethnographic area. But though my argument should not be treated as anything but a suggestive and preliminary statement, I think it better to submit it to prospective field-workers and students of magical facts.

In the first place, then, is it possible for us to venture on some general explanation of why the language of magic has this twofold character, why the coefficients of weirdness and intelligibility both dominate it. In the second place, the evolutionary or historical problem may have occurred to the reader. Have we to imagine that magical speech starts from sheer nonsense words and emotional sounds, or onomatopoetic reproduction of natural noises, and then develops towards an approximation to ordinary speech? Or should we adopt the inverse hypothesis that magical language at first is strictly utilitarian and rational in function, and gradually develops its weird and incomprehensible aspects? Or is there perhaps a still different genetic assumption to be made?

We have seen that language in its inception is both magical and pragmatic. It is charged with a mystical effectiveness and is used as a working tool. By "inception" we mean here, of course, the beginnings of speech in human life, rather than in the life of humanity. In so far as language is used in ordinary life, and for pragmatic purposes, the element of intelligibility comes to the fore. It reaches its maximum in the sociologically set language of drill, of cooperative speech used in economic enterprise. It reaches also its peak of pragmatic effectiveness in the technical terminology of arts and crafts by which the theory of manufacture is handed on from generation to generation and communication is possible between cooperating artisans. In so far as the same words and sentences are used with reference to emotional experiences and crystallized emotional attitudes belonging to the domain of magic and religion, these words and phrases are fraught with a meaning which has no roots in empirical experience or in cooperative activities. There, on the one hand, meaning becomes mystical, and on the other the forms become unusual in so far as they are no more adapted to ordinary communication. Within the linguistic theory of the present book, in which the distinction between "form" and meaning is in the last instance illusory, because form is sound within context, and meaning is the effect of sound within context, the twofold character of speech has nothing really mysterious or unexpected. We realize that all language in its earliest function within the context of infantile helplessness is proto-magical and pragmatic. It is pragmatic in that it works through the appeal to the child's human surroundings; it is proto-magical in that it contains all the emotional dependence of the child on those to whom it appeals through sound. In the course of long years, during which the pragmatic attitude towards words only gradually develops, the child experiences the power of words and sounds, especially when these are fraught with emotion as well as with the conventional significances of articulation.

Our theoretical approach thus supplies the answer to both questions in one hypothesis, that is, if we adopt the principle that the development of speech in humanity must have, in its fundamental principles, been of the same type as the development of speech within the life history of the individual. This I hold to be the only sound scientific approach to the genetic problems of language as also of other aspects of culture.

The thesis then which I am putting forward here is that the Trobriand phenomenon of a language of magic, within which we find a masquerading of significant speech under the guise of esoteric and mysterious forms, fits into the theory of language. In Trobriand magic we find hardly a single word, the working of which, that is, the meaning of which, could not be explained on the basis of associations, mythological data or some other aspect of Frazer's principle of sympathy. This, I think, is but part of the universal, essentially human, attitude of all men to all words. From the very use of speech men develop the conviction that the knowledge of a name, the correct use of a verb, the right application of a particle, have a mystical power which transcends the mere utilitarian convenience of such words in communication from man to man.

The child actually exercises a quasi-magical influence over its surroundings. He utters a word, and what he needs is done for him by his adult entourage. This is a point of view on which I do not need to enlarge. I think that the contributions of such modern child psychologists as Piaget and Bühler, and of older workers such as William Stern, supply us with a rich material for the confirmation of this point of view. But I have not been able to consult their work in connection with the writing of this division.

I have also stressed already the fact that this early attitude is partly superseded, but to a large extent confirmed in the further development of the individual. The mastery over reality, both technical and social, grows side by side with the knowledge of how to use words. Whether you watch apprenticeship in some craft within a primitive community or in our own society, you always see that familiarity with the name of a thing is the direct outcome of familiarity with how to use this thing. The right word for an action, for a trick of trade, for an ability, acquires *meaning* in the measure in which the individual becomes capable to carry out this action. The belief that to know the name of a thing is to get a hold on it is thus empirically true. At the same time, it lends itself to obvious distortions in the direction of mysticism. For the genuineness of the process, that is the genuineness of verbal power over things through manual and intellectual control, is the result of a fine balance. On the one hand we have people who are more effective manually than verbally. This is a handicap. The simple mind, primitive or civilized, identifies difficulty of speech and clumsiness and unreadiness of expression with mental deficiency. In the Trobriands *tonagowa* covers idiocy and defective speech; and among European peasantry the village idiot is very often merely a person who stammers or suffers from inability of clear expression. On the other hand the verbal type and the theoretical type of person surpass in mastery of words while they are backward in manual effectiveness. Even within the most primitive differentiation of activities the man who is better at counsel and advice, at talking and bragging, represents what in more advanced communities will become the schoolman, the talmudist or the baboo. This may be an unhealthy development of learning or of a purely consulting or advisory capacity; but it is rooted in something which functions throughout all human work—I mean the fact that some people must command, advise, plan and coordinate.

So far I have been mainly speaking about arts and crafts. Power through speech in the mastery of social relations, of legal rules and of economic realities, is quite as plain. The child who grows up in a primitive community and becomes instructed gradually in the intricacies of kinship, the taboos, duties and privileges of kindred, of clansmen, of people of higher and lower rank, learns the handling of social relations through the knowledge of sociological terms and phrases. The instruction may take place in the course of initiation ceremonies, a great part of which consists in the sociological apprenticeship of the child, boy or girl, youth or maiden, to tribal citizenship. But obviously there is a long educational process between the small infant, who can name and call for the few people of its immediate surroundings, and the adult tribesman or tribeswoman, who must address a score, a few hundred or even a few thousand people in the proper manner, appeal to them through adequate praise, be able to greet, converse and transact business with them. This process again has two sides: experience in "deportment," manners, practices and abstentions, and the capacity to name, describe and anticipate these things, and also to use the adequate words in these relations. Here also the mastery of social aspect and social terminology runs parallel.

If space allowed, I could enlarge on this side of our subject indefinitely. Take, for instance, the problem of law in its verbal and pragmatic aspects. Here the value of the word, the binding force of a formula, is at the very foundation of order and reliability in human relations. Whether the marriage vows are treated as a sacrament or as a mere legal contract—and in most human societies they have this twofold character—the power of words in establishing a permanent human relation, the sacredness of words and their socially sanctioned inviolability, are absolutely necessary to the existence of social order. If legal phrases, if promises and contracts were not regarded as something more than *flatus vocis*, social order would cease to exist in a complex civilization as well as in a primitive tribe. The average man, whether civilized or primitive, is not a sociologist. He neither needs to, nor can, arrive at the real function of a deep belief in the sanctity of legal and sacral words and their creative power. But he must have this belief; it is drilled into him by the process whereby he becomes part and parcel of the orderly institutions of his community. The stronger this belief, the greater becomes what might be called the elementary honesty and veracity of the citizens. In certain walks of human life speech may develop into the best instrument for the concealment of thought. But there are other aspects—law, contracts, the formulas of sacraments, oaths —in which a complicated apparatus inviolably based on mystical and religious ideas develops in every community as a necessary by-product of the working of legal and moral institutions and relation-ships.

This must suffice to establish my proposition that there is a very real basis to human belief in the mystic and binding power of words. We can also see where the truth of this belief really lies. Man rises above his purely animal, anatomical and physiological equip-ment by building up his culture in cooperation with his fellow be-ings. He masters his surroundings because he can work with others and through others. Verbal communication from the earliest infan-tile dependence of the child on his parents to the developed uses of full citizenship, scientific speech and words of command and leader-ship, is the correlate of this. The knowledge of right words, appro-priate phrases and the more highly developed forms of speech, gives man a power over and above his own limited field of personal action. But this power of words, this cooperative use of speech is and must be correlated with the conviction that a spoken word is sacred. The fact also that words add to the power of man over and above their strictly pragmatic effectiveness must be correlated with the belief that words have a mystical influence.

This sociological explanation of the belief in the mystical power of words is obviously a reinterpretation of Durkheim's theory that mysticism is but an expression in belief of man's dependence on society. But I think that Durkheim's theory is itself a somewhat mystical act of faith—in fact, it is little more than a reformation of the Hegelian doctrine of the Absolute, which embodies itself in the more and more perfectly organized human community. What I am trying to contribute here is a reinterpretation of Durkheimianism in empirical terms. Durkheim's basic conception that a great many phenomena in culture, belief and emotional attitude have to be accounted for by the fact that man is dependent on his fellow beings and that this dependence produces certain attitudes and leads to certain beliefs, is in my opinion fundamentally sound. Where Durk-heim "goes off the rails," so to speak, is in reducing his sound con-ception to a very narrow formula of the direct emotional experience of the crowd and of the influences of crowd phenomena on the in-dividual. He personified society himself, and he attributed this per-sonification to primitive man. Hence his simple formula that God is society, that the substance of the Absolute is nothing but the feeling of dependence which man, intoxicated by the dionysiac influence of a religiously effervescent crowd concretizes into sacred entities and sacred beings. There is no doubt that a *churinga* or a national flag, the cross or the crescent, plays an important part in the crystallizing of human attitudes. But to attribute to these phenomena of material symbolization, which take birth in an orgiastic crowd, the leading part in all cultural process is an extraordinary exaggeration. Durkheim, I think, caricatured his own theory in his biggest work on the Elementary Forms of Religious Belief.

The influence of society, or as I would prefer to say, the influence of culture—that is, of all the institutions found within a community, of the various traditional mechanisms such as speech, technology, mode of social intercourse—this influence works on the individual by a gradual process of molding. By this process of molding I mean the effect of traditional cultural modes and norms upon the growing organism. In one way the whole substance of my theory of culture, as I have sketched it out in my article on "Culture" (in the *Encyclopaedia of Social Sciences*), consists in reducing Durkheimian theory to terms of Behavioristic psychology.

Let me return to the subject in question. Having established the twofold aspect of linguistic development, the sacred and the profane, the mystical and the pragmatic, within the growth of every individual, we should find within every culture a ready-made distinction and traditional cleavage between these two aspects of human speech. In other words, having started by using language in a manner which is both magical and pragmatic, and passed gradually through stages in which the magical and pragmatic aspects intermingle and oscillate, the individual will find within his culture certain crystallized, traditionally standardized types of speech, with the language of technology and science at the one end, and the language of sacrament, prayer, magical formula, advertisement and political oratory at the other.

Thus if my theory is true, we ought to find in our own culture as well as in any other, these two poles of linguistic effectiveness, the magical and the pragmatic. Is this so? A digression on the modern language of magic would be very tempting, but I can only jot down one or two suggestions. Perhaps the best example of modern magical use of words is what might be called direct suggestion. Monsieur Coué has developed a technique as well as a theory, founded on this phenomenon. I have curative formulas from Trobriand magic which are based on exactly the principles of the Nancy school.

> It passes, it passes,
> The breaking pain in thy bones passes,
> The ulceration of thy skin passes,
> The big black evil of thy abdomen passes,
> It passes, it passes. . . .

Or take one of our formulas of garden magic:

> I sweep away, I sweep away, I sweep away.
> The grubs I sweep, I sweep away;
> The blight I sweep, I sweep away;
> Insects I sweep, I sweep away. . . .
> I blow, I blow, I blow away.
> The grubs I blow, I blow away;
> The blights I blow, I blow away;
> Insects I blow, I blow away. . . .

If instead of analyzing the doctrines of Monsieur Coué, which are based on a scientific point of view, we take the beliefs of Christian Science—the main root of which is that by affirming health, welfare, order and happiness generally, you produce them; and by denying them, by allowing evil thoughts to be rampant, you generate disease —we would have a very close parallel to the practices and beliefs of Trobriand sorcery and, I venture to say, of primitive sorcery in general. This subject, however, I must leave for the doctor's thesis of some young anthropologist, eager for parallels between modern and primitive savagery—parallels, which, I venture to foretell, would reward beyond the hopes of intellectual avarice. If we wanted to make an excursion into modern medical quackery, we could analyze the famous electric box and the magical verbiage which surrounded it; we could even attack some of the universal cures by cold water, fresh air, real or artificial sunlight, scrutinizing especially the advertisements emanating from such one-track remedies. But here again an indication must suffice.

And this brings me to perhaps the richest field of modern verbal magic, the subject of advertisements. The psychology of advertisement has been widely treated. One of the most prominent psychologists is a professional advertiser—I do not mean self-advertiser, but a member of an advertising firm. The subtle and witty analysis of verbal magic by Miss Dorothy Sayers in her detective story *Murder Must Advertise* would supply ample material for a doctor's thesis written by one who is also professionally connected with the advertising business. The advertisements of modern beauty specialists, especially of the magnitude of my countrywoman Helena Rubinstein, or of her rival, Elisabeth Arden, would make interesting reading if collated with the formulas of Trobriand beauty magic, reproduced in Chapter XIII of *Argonauts of the Western Pacific* and in Chapter XI of *Sexual Life of Savages*.

> I smooth out, I improve, I whiten.
> Thy head I smooth out, I improve, I whiten.
> Thy cheeks I smooth out, I improve, I whiten.
> Thy nose I smooth out, I improve, I whiten.
> Thy throat I smooth out, I improve, I whiten.
> Thy neck I smooth out, I improve, I whiten. . . .

The language of Trobriand magic is simpler, more direct and more honest, but it contains all the essentials of a good advertisement. Some of the formulas might indeed fall within the law of fair advertisement:

> One red paint of my companions,
> It is sere, it is parched. . . .
> One red paint, my red paint,
> It is clean, it is buoyant, it is flashing
> My red paint.

This phraseology might not be allowed to Monsieur Coty of Paris if he wanted to criticize the lipsticks produced by the Erasmic Co. of London. But similar implications run throughout modern advertisements.

Side by side with advertisement, modern political oratory would probably yield a rich harvest of purely magical elements. Some of the least desirable of modern pseudo-statesmen or gigantic politicanti have earned the titles of wizards or spell-binders. The great leaders such as Hitler or Mussolini have achieved their influence primarily by the power of speech, coupled with the power of action which is always given to those who know how to raise the prejudices and the passions of the mob. Moreover, the modern socialistic state, whether it be painted red, black, or brown, has developed the powers of advertisement to an extraordinary extent. Political propaganda, as it is called, has become a gigantic advertising agency, in which merely verbal statements are destined to hypnotize foreigner and citizen alike into the belief that something really great has been achieved.

With this indictment of modern savagery I must close these desultory remarks, which should not be treated as on the same plane with the rest of this contribution. In my opinion the study of mod-

ern linguistic uses side by side with those of the magic of simple
peoples would bring high rewards. At the very basis of verbal magic
there lies what I have elsewhere called "the creative metaphor of
magic." By this I mean that the repetitive statement of certain words
is believed to produce the reality stated. I think that if we stripped
all magical speech to its essentials, we would find simply this fact:
a man believed to have mystical powers faces a clear blue sky and
repeats: "It rains; dark, clouds forgather; torrents burst forth and
drench the parched soil." Or else he would be facing a black sky
and repeat: "The sun breaks through the clouds; the sun shines."
Or in illness he repeats, like Monsieur Coué: "Every day and in
every way it is getting better and better." The essence of verbal
magic, then, consists in a statement which is untrue, which stands
in direct opposition to the context of reality. But the belief in magic
inspires man with the conviction that his untrue statement must
become true. How far this is rooted in emotional life, in the power
of man to daydream, in unconquerable human hopes and human
optimism, is clear to those who are acquainted with the fact of magic
as well as with the theoretical literature connected with it. In another place also I have defined magic as the institutionalized expression of human optimism, of constructive hopes overcoming
doubt and pessimism.

I would like to add here that when Freud defines this function of
magic as the "omnipotence of thought" (*Allmacht der Gedanken*)
and tries to find the roots of magical activities in the human tendency
idly to daydream, this view requires a serious correction—a correction which is contained in our theory here. Because—and this is of
the greatest importance—man never runs on the sidetrack of magical
verbiage or of magical activities in that idle daydreaming which
stultifies action. Organized magic always appears within those domains of human activity where experience has demonstrated to man
his pragmatic impotence. In the measure as humanity, through developing technique, conquers one realm of activity after another,
magic disappears and is replaced by science and technique. We do
not use magic in agriculture any more, we do not attract shoals of
fish by magic nor improve the trajectory of a high explosive by incantations. Aspects of human activity which have been made subject to the control of physics, chemistry or biology, are treated by
systems based on reason and experience. And even in primitive
communities we find a clear realization of those phases in fishing,
hunting and agriculture which are mastered by man with his im-
plements, his hands and his brains; where man knows that his

thought is impotent, there and there only does he resort to magic. Magic is not a belief in the omnipotence of thought but rather the clear recognition of the limitations of thought, nay, of its impotence. Magic, more especially verbal magic, grows out of legitimate uses of speech, and it is only the exaggeration of one aspect of these legitimate uses. More than that: ritual magic and verbal magic are not mere counterparts of idle daydreaming. In the affirmation of the hopeful aspect magic exercises an integrative influence over the individual mind. Through the fact that this integrative influence is also connected with an organizing power, magic becomes also an empirical force. Freud's conception of magic as a type of vicious megalomania would relegate it to the domain of cultural pathology. Frazer's theory that sympathetic magic is due to a mistaken association of ideas, while it explains one aspect of magic, namely the sympathetic principle which underlies the creative metaphor of magic, still does not account for the enormous organizing part played by magic. Durkheim's view that the substance of magic, that is *mana* or magical force, is nothing but society personified, explains one mystical attitude by inviting us to assume another.

In my opinion magic has exercised a profound positive function in organizing enterprise, in inspiring hope and confidence in the individual. Side by side with this magical belief has obviously developed an attitude which exerts disturbing and subversive influences, especially in witchcraft and black magic. In the history of culture every phenomenon, I think, has got its constructive and disintegrating sides, its organizing functions and its influences which point towards dissolution and decay. Human cultures do not merely grow and develop. They also decompose, die or collapse. Functional anthropology is not magic; it is not a chartered optimism or whitewashing of culture. One of its duties, in the wider cultural sense, is to show that savagery and superstition are not confined to primitive society. If we have insisted on the "white" aspects of magic side by side with its black aspects, it is rather to bring into relief something which has been less fully recognized and elaborated in anthropological literature and in the practical approach to facts. Apart from Frazer's work on *Psyche's Task* (reprinted as the *Devil's Advocate*), the constructive side of magic has not been sufficiently recognized; and even now, when formulated, it meets with vigorous opposition—remarkably enough from the modern theologian.[1]

[1] Cf. the criticism of some of my views by Dean Inge in his concluding article in *Science, Religion and Reality*, Joseph Needham (London: The Sheldon Press, 1925).

In the general digression just concluded, I have laid stress on the organizing function of magic. Let me exemplify this on our Trobriand material, and show how this side of magical phenomena directly influences the wording of spells. Let us once more listen to the Trobriand magician while he addresses spirits and animals, plants and soil. The spell in the belief of the natives is a verbal communion between the magician and the object addressed. The magician speaks and the objects respond. The words are launched into the things—sometimes even the surrounding world gives the sign that the words have been received by the essence of things: the *kariyala,* "magical portent," awakens, the thunder rumbles in the skies and lightning appears on the horizon. But once we understand that while the magician addresses animals and plant agents, while he launches his words towards the soil and the tubers, these words are believed to take effect, then we realize that by this very belief they do have an affect. On whom? Not on the soil and spirits, on the spider and the full moon. This is a native belief which, important as it is, does not directly bind us. But—and this is of the highest importance to the sociologist—they do really produce an effect on the magician himself, on his retinue and on all those who work with him, under him, and by him. It is the sociological setting which is of the greatest importance in the study of magic, because it is this indirect effect of the words upon the psychology or physiology of the native organism, and hence upon social organization, which probably gives us the best clue to the nature of magical meaning. It also furnishes us, in connection with the data supplied by native belief, with the real answer to the question: What have we to do in translating magical words?

The words which are meant for things that have no ears fall upon ears they are not meant for. It is the influence of magic on the community practicing it which molds ritual and language, which influences the selection of substances, the gestures and the words. We have asked rhetorically whether, in mumbling his incantations over the herbs in his hut, in addressing the spirits, in chanting his spell into a tuber or a sapling or a plot, the magician talks simply in monologue? The answer is now clear. When a man mumbles or chants to himself while at work for his own pleasure, the work would not suffer greatly if he were silenced. But if the magician were to stop in his solitary mumblings a complete disorganization of the work of the whole community would follow.

The reader who has attentively perused the foregoing descriptive chapters will fully appreciate this and needs no further argument. Throughout our account we saw how, at every step, the magician and his art formed the main organizing force in gardening. We have also seen that the *towosi* is the leader, initiating and supervising the successive activities, because he wields the *mana* which ultimately resides in words. But before he can use the words he must be in the right matrilineal lineage, and receive the magic from his predecessor in a socially and ritually correct manner. This process itself presents certain complications into which we need not enter here; but the essentials are that the magician must learn the words accurately, submit to all taboos imposed by his office and be officially approved by his predecessor, usually after the presentation of ceremonial gifts.

How far is all this associated with the words of magic? This question brings us directly to the more elementary one: How far do members of the community at large know the words, and how far are they aware of the spells? The answer to this is that every member of the community is aware of each spell being performed; that down almost to the children they are familiar with the wording of each spell, and regard its recitation as the most important part, not merely in the big ceremonial performance which surrounds it, but in the whole sequence of general activities.

It will be best, perhaps, to illustrate this social, economic, and generally cultural context of spells on the first formula which we meet. This formula is uttered in the magician's house, while he offers some particles of food to the spirits. The performance itself seems extremely private, detached from the rest of social activities, and relatively unsuitable to affect either the minds of the natives or to organize their behavior.

Let us, however, consider what has gone before; first of all the offering of the particles of fish to the spirits has to be prepared. The men have twice gone on special expeditions to the coast in order to procure fish. They offered this fish to the magician as *ula'ula* payment; the word itself, *ula'ula*, which means both "ceremonial payment" and "oblation to the spirits," indicates that the offering is to the spirits as well as to the magician. This latter has, on the morning of the same day, gone out to gather the magical herbs from which he will prepare the magical mixture. The men meanwhile have made ready their axes for the ritual benediction of magic which will be uttered over them.

Thus the whole community shares in the preparations for this, the crucial and essential act, the utterance of the two consecutive formulas. The rite itself is, so to speak, the goal of all the previous activities, just as it is the condition of the whole ceremony that is performed on the morrow in the gardens.

After everything has been prepared the magician retires to his house and the other gardeners disperse. It is, moreover, not usual that anybody should be present with him in the house, although a younger brother or matrilineal nephew may assist at the rite, and would so assist at least once or twice when learning the magic.

But while the magician holds solitary communion with the spirits and later impregnates the herbs and axes with the most important vehicle of magical force, the *vatuvi* spell, the whole community is aware of what is happening under the thatch of the magician's hut. His voice, although he does not shout the words, can yet be heard within a radius of three- or fourscore feet or so, so that it reaches the inmates of the nearest houses. They hear him addressing the spirits. They know that he communes with them by the gift and through the words. They are made to realize that now the blessing of the ghosts of those who have once wielded the magic is being invoked. The affirmation of tradition dwells over the whole village. The *towosi* now becomes the representative of a long line of ancestors whom he first addresses as a whole and then enumerates by name. Some of the words uttered by him restate his charter. Some other words again are commentaries upon the importance of the *wasi*, i.e. the complex transaction by which fish is procured; on the *ula'ula*, the gift and the oblation, and on the anticipated magic. "Tomorrow we penetrate our garden-site" ("we" embracing the spirits, the magician, and the whole community).

And with all this every villager realizes that the words which produce such a powerful effect can be uttered by not one except the one who is sociologically determined as the right magician and who fulfills the mystical conditions of correct knowledge and full observance of the taboos.

The analysis of the sociological aspects of the next spell, which on this occasion is recited immediately after Formula 1, will show us that here also in the list of ancestors and in the mythological references the magician establishes the traditional charter. Again in the first words of blessing, in the anticipatory affirmations of plenty, in the declaration of his magical powers, which he achieves by speaking in the first person and by boldly uttering the affirmations and exorcisms of magic, he takes in hand the full fate of the gardens.

I must repeat that the natives are familiar with every spell. Although no unauthorized native would ever dare to utter a magical formula, unless at least potentially entitled by birth to do so, I discovered that there was not a single man in Omarakana who would not recognize a text belonging to his community's official magic. Most of the formula they hear once or even twice every year. As far as I could ascertain the formulas of growth magic, spoken as they are over each field, are usually witnessed and heard by a considerable number of people, although there is no official attendance. There are, however, other means by which the natives learn to know the formulas. In the first place there are several men in each community who are officially and openly instructed in this magic: besides the garden magician himself, his younger brothers and matrilineal nephews are taught the spells. Very often the older members of the family who, for some reason, do not practice this magic, yet know it thoroughly. Thus in Omarakana, besides Bagido'u, To'uluwa, the old chief, knew the magic quite well though, having a bad memory, he never could recite a spell from beginning to end; so did two or three *tabalu* from the neighboring village of Kasana'i. Thus Tokolibeba, Kwaywaya and old Mtabalu, when he was alive, knew every word in each formula. In Omarakana old Molubabeba knew this magic and recited it in the presence of his son Tokulubakiki, who once or twice helped me in translating a spell. Besides these, both the younger brothers of Bagido'u, Towese'i and Mitakata, had already learned it. Now every one of these people was quite at liberty to comment privately upon any part of this magic to his relatives or friends. For let us remember that there is no taboo at all on divulging the magic or even reciting it privately and with discretion—provided that you have the hereditary right to do so. Thus the magic percolates, so to speak, so that practically everybody in the village knows it. We know also that there are official occasions on which the practicing magician himself will recite the magic aloud, notably during the mortuary vigil over any important person.

We can now approach the real problem before us: how to translate a magical utterance, how to bring home the real meaning of a meaningless, or at least distorted, word. We will start from the point which I have just been making, namely, that the words of magic are familiar to all the community, that they are listened to or that there is at least a keen awareness and appreciation of their utterance. So that in spite of a pretence of privacy and strict monopoly of use the spell is, in the sense here elaborated, the concern of those for whom it is enacted.

How far does this affect our problem? If each and all the words which form a spell are of importance not merely to the spirits and magical forces, but to the natives themselves, it becomes clear that the verbal substance of the spells is correlated with the mental outlook of the natives. The magician in uttering his formulas speaks on behalf of each gardener. He expresses what each gardener feels, hopes for and anticipates. But magic in its essence, I might almost say in its physiological essence, is the expression of human hope and confidence, of the need of a morally integrated attitude towards the future.

This as we know is fully confirmed by the general theory of magical words here developed; this also agrees with the verbal facts which we have observed. As we have already seen, and as we shall see more clearly in the texts and commentaries which follow, most of the crucial words of Trobriand magic, the key words of the main part, the leading words which run throughout the whole spell, the initial words which characterize a formula, are words of blessing, anticipatory affirmations of prosperity and plenty, exorcisms of evil influences, and mythological references which draw upon the strength of the past for the welfare of the future. The words which we find in magic are the equivalents of what in personal language we would find expressing the hopes of each individual, his confidence in the power of his magician to see himself and his fellows through a bad season, his conviction that the magic is an ultimate stand-by against adversity.

When in the second formula the magician utters the word *vatuvi*, whatever may emerge from its analysis, this word certainly expresses a general blessing, a blessing which, as determined by its context, is meant to go into the depths, into the body of the earth and become anchored there. This word has been heard for generations in Omarakana and stands to the natives for the value and importance of their agriculture in general and for the special greatness of their own garden magic which, let us remember, is that of the premier community of the Trobriands.

When in the other great formula of garden magic, he uses as leading word one which expresses the idea of anchoring, very permanently mooring, and repeats this word with the expressions for the fundamental parts of the "magical wall," he again establishes, in this verbal act, the stability of the garden. The same obviously holds good of this spell when uttered with appropriate variations over the storehouses. Thus the affirmation of stability runs through a great many formulas, for the examples here given could be multiplied.

In other spells the magician invokes fertility in general, as, for instance, in the second spell when he bursts into an anticipatory vision of all that the belly of the garden will bring forth; or again when he foretells the rising of the crops, or describes, in tensely figurative speech, the flame-like bursting of the garden towards the village and towards the jungle; or when he describes the size of the taro. Growth magic especially is characterized by such hopeful anticipations and affirmations. Each phase of growing and development is stated in an exaggerated manner with repetitions of "new" and of "old," of morning and evening, of north and south, of one end of the district and another. The strange exaggerations which we find in a number of formulas—the vomiting from surfeit of taytu, the groaning under the weight of the crops, the death from surfeit—all these express the craving of the gardeners for success, for prosperity, for *malia,* and their belief that by verbal statements all they crave for can be realized. When the magician verbally summons various natural forces to help him, when he uses the negative exaggerations which have been so often mentioned, and speaks about many canoesful of taytu, we meet with the same creative function of speech. To use our former expression, we could say that the creative metaphor of magic dominates throughout the ritual language of Trobriand spells.

It is clear that the words of this type, words which are obviously expressions of strong desire, words the primary function of which is, from the standpoint of individual psychology, to create confidence, to enhance hopes and anticipations, and thus to stimulate people to effort, perseverance and energy, cannot be treated as direct communications or definitions. The mystical words of blessing, of plenty, of stability, and again the strong imperatives of exorcism, must be treated rather as verbal acts which radiate emotional influence, which reproduce feeling, which carry with them a wide system of associations.

The indirect function of such words, then, consists in their influence on the psychology of each individual of the community. But this influence does not remain merely individual. It is one of the powerful elements which contribute towards the integration of the villagers into an effective gardening team.

Thus the fact that the community is aware of the spell and knows its wording is the most important clue to the appreciation of the verbalities of magic—that is, if we realise that such a cultural phenomenon as spoken magic is of slow growth, that it is shaped gradually through the various mental and social forces which work upon it; above all, that the ultimate *raison d'être* of its fundamental characters must be correlated with its function. In other words since, in my opinion, the spell plays an important part in influencing individuals in their agricultural work; since it plays this part because of the characteristics which I have just enumerated, I am convinced that we have arrived at an explanation also of the process by which these characteristics came into being.

Let us follow this out a little more in detail in a frankly evolutionary or historical hypothesis as to the origins of magic. The "ultimate origins," as I have said in a previous division, were probably the affirmations of ordinary speech, what we have there called the simplest creative metaphors of magic. These are crystallized into a set formula and chanted with the characteristic emotional intonations of magic. And now comes into being the cultural apparatus of magic, consisting in its sociological side of the leader, who performs the rite and chants the spell, and of the members of the community, who can hear the spell and are aware that magic is being carried out on their behalf. But it is not merely the audience who are aware of the magician; the magician is also aware of his audience. He knows that he is uttering it on behalf of his fellow workers; he voices their pride in their magic (*da megwa-si*); he shares their belief in its efficacy, for he bears the responsibility of being the leader.

But—and here comes the historically important fact—the psychology of the individual magician is not a circumstance which lies idle and ineffective, separated from his activity as magician. The most important fact is that in each generation the spell, its explanatory comments, its mythological matrix, and the whole technique of its recital are in the possession of the magician in office. This official magician has to transmit his formulas with the associated magical lore to his successor. In so doing he acts not merely as a passive receptacle of tradition, he is also the leader of his community, their spokesman, the repository of all their beliefs, hopes, anticipations, and strivings. In every generation, therefore, the carrying out of the magic—and that means not merely the recital of the spells, but their explanation and traditional handling—will be influenced by the general attitude of the community towards the spells as part of the magic. This attitude is a controlling force of what a magician thinks and feels, says and does. This controlling force will show its influence above all in the process, repeated generation after generation, in fact, several times within each generation, by which magic is handed over from elder to younger brother, from uncle to maternal nephew, occasionally from father to son.

We can now deal with our conundrum about the meaning of

meaningless words in magic. First of all we have been able to establish the fact that these words are meaningless only it we let ourselves
be confused by the superficial distortions, by the clipped and unusual style of magic. These elements, as a matter of fact, have a
meaning in that they play a part. This part is determined by the
typical human attitude towards magical speech. In the Trobriands
the belief that spell words belong to a different category is definitely
correlated with the coefficient of weirdness which, as we have shown,
is more apparent than real. Spells remain meaningless also in so far
as we fail to connect them with their ritual context and to place
them against their mythology and dogmatics. Above all, and in connection with the point just made, we have clearly to recognize that,
since the function of magical speech is not to communicate ideas
or to narrate, the analysis has to be based on a full understanding
of the effects which the words produce. The function of a spell, that
is its meaning, has to be accounted for first of all in connection with
native belief. We have to establish then what in native belief is the
effect which the words and phrases exercise within the traditional
universe of magic upon the things or beings to be influenced. In
order to bring home this aspect of their meaning the ethnographer
has to state all the mystical, mythological, and traditional associations of the words.

To the ethnographer, however, the words of magic have another
significance, even more important than their mystical effects, and
that is the effect which the words of magic produce on human
beings. Here the ethnographer can and must go beyond what the
natives are able to tell him. He not only has to explore all possible
associations, but he has also to treat parts of the magical texts as
sociological charters, other parts as forms of suggestion, others again
as vehicles of hope and desire. We shall see that in some of the
spells the magician establishes his claim to be the rightful successor
to the magic, in others he gives evidence of his communion with
the spirits, in others he announces his power over animal agents,
factors of fertility, pests, blights, and bush-pigs. This aspect of verbal
magic is an essential part of its sociological function.

All this will be illustrated in the comments on the texts which
follow, especially in the comments on the really difficult words of
Formula 2. The first word there, *vatuvi*, is obviously one of those
expressions which do not refer to any specific object, but magically
grip an aspect of the whole situation. *Vatuvi* has no grammatical
form. It is neither noun nor verb, though by its etymological affini-
ties it is of a verbal character. An inaugurative word, it is launched

freely into the substances to be charmed, the herbs, the axes, the torches, and digging-sticks. It has got no context of direct connection with any specific thing or agency. It has to be taken as a verbal missile of magical power—a conception very much in harmony with the repetitive character of its utterance, whereby it is rubbed into the substance. Incidentally, the manner in which a spell is chanted has to be described in order that we may understand the full meaning of the word.

The word, therefore, will have to be treated not as a precise verbal statement, not as an imperative, nor as the naming of a thing, nor as any definite verbal form, but rather as a word rich in associations and reaching out in many directions. As we shall see, the real etymological identity of this word will define it as connected with *vitawo*, or the prefix *vitu-*, and the word *vituvatu*, "to institute," "to set up," "to direct," "to show." We shall also discuss its fortuitous, but magically significant associations with *vatu*, "coral boulder," "coral reef," and the more or less real word *va-tuvi*, "to foment," "to make heal."

The meaning of this word consists: (1) in the effect which it is believed to produce; (2) in the manner in which it is launched as regards ritual handling and general cultural setting; (3) in its etymological associations which show the influence which it exercises upon the mind of the magician and upon that of each member of the community; (4) in the possible sociological functions of such a word. In the case of *vatuvi* there is no direct sociological import such as we find in other words, but indirectly, since it is a general blessing and declaration of power, it influences the position of the magician and the relations of the community to him.

U and Non-U:
An Essay
in Sociological Linguistics

by ALAN S. C. ROSS

Today, in 1956, the English class system is essentially tri-partite—there exist an upper, a middle, and a lower class. It is solely by its language that the upper class is clearly marked off from the others. In times past (e.g. in the Victorian and Edwardian periods) this was not the case. But, today, a member of the upper class is, for instance, not necessarily better educated, cleaner, or richer than someone not of this class. Nor, in general, is he likely to play a greater part in public affairs, be supported by other trades or professions,[1] or engage in other pursuits or pastimes than his fellow of another class. There are, it is true, still a few minor points of life which may serve to demarcate the upper class,[2] but they are only

[1] It may, however, be doubted how far the Navy and the Diplomatic Service will in practice (in contradistinction to theory) be "democratized," even if there should be a succession of Labour Governments; foreigners seem to expect English diplomats to be of the upper class.

[2] In this article I use the terms *upper class* (abbreviated: U), *correct, proper, legitimate, appropriate* (sometimes also *possible*) and similar expressions (including some containing the word *should*) to designate usages of the upper class; their antonyms (*non-U, incorrect, not proper, not legitimate,* etc.) to designate usages which are not upper class. These terms are, of course, used factually and not in reprobation (indeed I may at this juncture emphasize a point which is doubtless obvious, namely that this whole article is purely factual). *Normal* means common both to U and non-U. I often use expressions such as *U-speaker* to denote a member of the upper class and, also, *gentleman,* pl. *gentlemen* (for brevity, in respect of either sex—the plural *gentlefolk* is no longer U). Class distinction is very dear to the heart of the upper class and talk about it is hedged with taboo. Hence, as in sexual matters, a large number of circumlocutions is used. Forty years ago, as I understand, U-speakers made use of *lady* and *gentleman* without self-consciousness; the antonym of *gentleman* was often *cad* or *bounder.* Today, save by older people, these terms can hardly be used to indicate class-distinction, for they sound either pedantic or facetious (*you cad, Sir!*). *Lady* and *gentleman*

minor ones. The games of real tennis and piquet,[3] an aversion to
high tea, having one's cards[4] engraved (not printed), not playing
tennis in braces, and, in some cases, a dislike of certain comparatively modern inventions such as the telephone, the cinema, and the
wireless are still perhaps marks of the upper class.[5] Again, when
drunk, gentlemen often become amorous or maudlin or vomit in
public, but they never become truculent.

In the present article I am concerned with the linguistic demarcation of the upper class. This subject has been but little investi-
gated, though it is much discussed, in an unscientific manner, by
members of that class. The late Professor H. C. Wyld wrote a short
article on the subject. He was well equipped for the task, for he was
both a gentleman and a philologist. Today, his views are perhaps a
little old-fashioned; for instance, the dictum "No gentleman goes on
a bus," attributed to him, is one which most gentlemen have to
neglect.

Both the written and the spoken language of the upper class serve
to demarcate it, but the former to only a very slight extent. A piece
of mathematics or a novel written by a member of the upper class
is not likely to differ in any way from one written by a member of
another class, except in so far as the novel contains conversation. In
writing, it is, in fact, only modes of address, postal addresses, and
habits of beginning and ending letters that serve to demarcate the
class.

------

have, of course, senses quite unconnected with class distinction, but, today, the
use of these words in the senses "man" and "woman" between U-speakers has
almost entirely vanished save when prefixed with *old* (*There's an old* LADY *to
see you* is different from *There's an old* WOMAN *to see you,* for the former implies
that the person is U, the latter that she is very non-U). *She's a nice lady* is
non-U, *He's a nice gentleman* even more so (*man, woman,* or *girl* being the
U-use here).

[3] But solo whist (or *solo* as its devotees call it) is non-U, though much "lower"
games (e.g. pontoon, nap, and even Slippery Sam) are not necessarily so. Whist
used to be a U-game but it, today, almost entirely confined to whist drives, which
are non-U (*they* STAND UP *to deal, my dear!*).

[4] The normal U-word is *card* (though this is ambiguous with (*playing*)-*card*).
Carte de visite was apparently U but would today seem unbearably old-fashioned.
Calling-card and *visiting-card* are non-U; the latter term is, in any case, an unfortunate one because of the non-U slang phrase *He's left his visiting-card* (of
a dog)—foreigners would do well to beware of "idiomatic" sentences such as
The Picts left their visiting-card in the Pentland Firth (said, in a public lecture,
meaning that the name *Pict* is preserved in the first element of *Pentland*).

[5] Certainly many U-speakers hunt—but hunting has for long been something
that the *nouveau riche* knows he should do in order to be U; many farmers
hunt too. So, today, hunting is not *ipso facto* a class-indicator.

Before proceeding to the detail of the present study I must emphasize that I am here concerned only with usages which serve to demarcate the upper class. The line of demarcation relevant to this study is, often, a line between, on the one hand, gentlemen and, on the other, persons who, though not gentlemen, might at first sight appear, or would wish to appear, as such. Thus, habits of speech peculiar to the lower classes find no place here. I may also note here that the U-demarcation is of two types: (1) a certain U-feature has a different, non-U, counterpart, as non-U *wealthy* = U *rich;* (2) a certain feature is confined to U-speech and it has a counterpart which is not confined to non-U speech, e.g. the pronunciations of *girl* to rhyme with *hell* and *Hal* are U, but many (perhaps most male) U-speakers, like all non-U-speakers, use the pronunciation that rhymes with *curl.*

The Written Language

The following points may be considered:
(1) Names on envelopes, etc.
(2) Beginnings of letters.
(3) Names on cards.
(4) Postal addresses on envelopes, etc., at the heads of letters, and on cards.
(5) Letter-endings.

Of these points the first three are mutually linked and the second —beginnings of letters—is linked with the spoken language; for, in general, a person known to the writer is written to and spoken to in the same mode of address. It will therefore be convenient to treat all modes of address together, though this means taking the spoken modes out of place.

Modes of address, particularly those used for the nobility, have always been a bugbear to the non-U. It is, for instance, non-U to speak of an earl as *The Earl of P*—; he should be spoken of and to as *Lord P*—and also so addressed at the beginning of a letter if an introduction between him and the speaker/writer has been effected. If the acquaintance is close, *P*—should be used instead of *Lord P*—. Letters to baronets and knights to whom one has been introduced should begin *Dear Sir A—X—*[6] if the acquaintance is slight, *Dear Sir A*—if it is not slight. In speaking *to* one, only *Sir A*—is possible.

---

[6] *A*—, *B*—, *C*—, etc. are christian names (the initials being written *A.*, *B.*, *C.*, etc.); *X*—is a surname.

In speaking *of* one, *Sir A*—should not be used unless the acquaintance is fairly close, *Sir A—X—*, or *X—*, being correct. If the acquaintance is slight or non-existent, the use of *Sir A*—in speaking
of a baronet or knight is non-U and "snobbish" [7] as attempting to
raise the social tone of the speaker. Letters to ambassadors whom
one does not know should begin *Dear Excellency* and the envelope
should be addressed *H. E. The P—Ambassador*. In speech, a Lieu-
tenant-Commander is addressed as *Commander,* a Lieutenant in the
Army as *Mister*. In concluding this section it may be noted that, in
writing letters to noblemen of very high rank, the rules laid down
in the etiquette-books[8] need not always be strictly observed. Thus
a Duke addressed by a stranger as *Dear Sir* would not necessarily
conclude that his correspondent was non-U; he might be a left-wing
gentleman with a dislike of dukedoms.

On envelopes, gentlemen put *Esq*. after the names of persons who
are, or who might wish to be considered, gentlemen, whether in fact
armigerous or not. *Esq*. is, however, not used on oneself, e.g. neither
on a card (which bears *Mr*.) nor on a stamped-and-addressed envelope enclosed for a reply (which has merely *A—B. X—* or *A. B. X*
—without prefix). Knowledge of at least one initial of the recipient's
name is, of course, a prerequisite for addressing him with *Esq*. If
the writer has not this minimum knowledge (and cannot, or is too
lazy to obtain it) he will be in a quandary. In these circumstances
I myself use the Greek letter Θ (as *Θ. Smith, Esq.*), but this is probably idiosyncratic. But to address someone as " *—Smith," Esq*. is
not so much non-U as definitely rude.[9] Gentlemen usually address
non-U males as *Mr.;* in internal circulation (e.g. in Government
offices), gentlemen may address each other in this way. Schoolboys
at their preparatory school (and younger boys) should be addressed

---

[7] "Snobs" are of two kinds; *true snobs* (Thackeray's kind) and *inverted snobs*.
Both kinds respect a person the more the better bred he is. True snobs indicate
this in their behavior to, and in their conversation about, persons of good family, though they do not usually admit this. In their conversation about (but not
in their behavior to) such persons, inverted snobs indicate that they respect a
person the less the better bred he is. One would expect to find a third category:
those who really do respect a person the less the better bred he is, and indicate
it. But this third category does not appear to exist. Nearly all English people
are snobs of one of the two kinds (in this respect England differs from Finland
and Iceland and resembles Spain and pre-War Hungary). And, just as it is impossible to find someone exactly half male and half female, so it is impossible
to find an Englishman in whom true and inverted snobbery exactly balance.

[8] It is, of course, very non-U actually to consult these.

[9] I may note here that many U-speakers omit the *Esq*. on checks.

as *Master;* at their public school, merely as *A. B. X*—(without prefix or suffix). The non-U usually address all adult males as *Mr.,* but tradespeople have copied the use of *Esq.* from their customers. Those gentlemen who are inverted snobs dislike *Esq.,* but, since they know that to address someone as *Mr.* is non-U, they avoid this also and address all adult males without prefix or suffix (like the correct mode of address for public school boys). Intellectuals, of any class, often begin letters, even where the acquaintance is slight, with *Dear A—X—.*

Postal addresses. It is non-U to place the name of a house in inverted commas (as *"Fairmeads")* or to write the number in full, either without or (especially) with inverted commas (*as Two, —worse "Two,"—St. Patrick's Avenue*). The names of many houses are themselves non-U; the ideal U-address is *P—Q—, R—,* where *P*—is a place-name, *Q*—a describer, and *R*—the name (or abbreviation) of a county as *Shinwell Hall, Salop.*[10] But, today, few gentlemen can maintain this standard and they often live in houses with non-U names such as *Fairmeads* or *El Nido.*

Letter-endings. The U-rules for ending letters are very strict; failure to observe them usually implies non-U-ness, sometimes only youth. In general, the endings of letters are conditioned by their beginnings. Thus a beginning (*Dear*) *Sir*[11] requires the ending *Yours faithfully,* unless the writer hopes to meet the recipient when *Yours very truly* may be used. Acquaintances who begin letters with *Dear Mr. X*—sign them *Yours sincerely* or *Yours very sincerely;* perversely, the latter ending is less cordial than the former. People who know each other really well will begin *Dear A*—or *Dear X*—(males only) and sign *Yours ever.* The ending *Yours* is often used even by gentlemen if they are in doubt as to which ending is appropriate.

The name after the letter ending offers little scope for comment. Letters are perhaps most usually signed in such forms as *A—X—, A—B. X—, A. B—X*—(the choice between the two last depending upon which christian name the writer is normally called by). If the writer is unknown (or not well known) to the recipient, the latter

---

[10] Here I may note a curious indicator. In speaking, it is, in general, non-U to use the whole name of such a house as in *I'm going to Shinwell Hall* (the U-sentence would be *I'm going to Shinwell*)—this obtains whether the house belongs to the speaker (or his relatives) or not.

[11] Whether the writer is U or not, this is the normal beginning of all business letters to unknowns; the variant *Sir* is correctly used to Government officials, *Sire* (or *Your Majesty*) to kings; *My Dear Sir* is felt as American.

cannot know whether the former is plain *Mr.* (if male), *Miss, Mrs.,*
or something else (if female); it is therefore usual for the writer to
inform the recipient if he is other than plain *Mr.* (if male), other
than *Miss* (if female). In handwritten letters, a usual way of doing
this is to sign as, for instance, (*Professor*) *A—B. X—*; in typewritten
letters (*Professor A—B. X—*) may be typed below the handwritten
signature *A—B. X—*. I have seen long titles (e.g. *Dowager Countess
of*) appended as footnotes to the signature. In concluding this section I may mention that people sometimes sign themselves (or enter
their names in lists, etc.) with the surname only; this usage is very
non-U, the reason for its non-U-ness lying in the fact that the correct
signature of peers is of this form (e.g. the Earl of P—signs himself
just *P—*).[12]

Here I may refer to R. W. Chapman's excellent *Names, designations & appellations,* published in 1946. [13] The author states (p. 231)
that the work is "an attempt to describe the modern use, in good
society in this country, of personal names and designations, spoken
or written, in the second or third person." [14] Chapman does not
specifically deal with non-U usages but, since his enumeration is intended as exhaustive, it may be assumed that, essentially, usages
divergent from those given by him are non-U, except in so far as
I have dealt with them.

I may comment on certain points mentioned by Chapman where
the usage of 1956 differs from that of a rather old-fashioned person
writing some years earlier. I arrange the commentary by the pages
of his book, either citing passages therefrom in quotation marks,
or (where this would be too lengthy) indicating in square brackets
[" "] the point under discussion.

pp. 237-8. ["Spouse: third person."] The mode in which a speaker
refers to his spouse is markedly distinct as between U- and non-U-
speakers. A U-speaker, naming his wife to an equal, normally says
My wife (or uses her christian name); to a very non-U person he says
Mrs. X—. Chapman says (p. 237) of a U-speaker referring to the
hearer's wife [" 'Your wife' may be over-familiar if I do not know
Jones (i.e. the hearer) very well"]. He advocates the use, then, of

---

[12] The correct form of postcards differs slightly from that of letters, for both
the beginning (*Dear A—*, etc.) and the ending (*Yours sincerely,* etc.) are omitted.
Some U-speakers feel it wrong to sign a postcard to a friend by anything save
the bare initial(s) (*A.* or *A. B. X.*).

[13] S. P. E. Tract No. XLVII.

[14] By the "second person" he means speaking *to* a person, by the "third person,"
speaking *of* one.

Mrs. Jones. Actually, I think that, of recent years, there has been a considerable increase in the use of *Your wife, Your husband* by U-speakers, even in cases where the acquaintance is of the slightest. Non-U-speakers do not in general make use of *my/your wife/husband*, preferring *Mr./Mrs. X—*.

p. 238. [" 'What does Weston think of the weather?', Mr. Knightly asked Mrs. Weston. But I should be chary of following this precedent."] I agree with Chapman. There is, however, rather a similar case, not mentioned by Chapman (doubtless because it is a very minor one), where surnames may be used. Schoolboys and young men frequently refer to each other by their surnames, so parents of a boy, talking to one of his acquaintances, often use the acquaintance's surname because they do not know his christian name; similarly, the acquaintance may call the son by his surname to the parents. It is not until a boy gets older (c. 16?) that he realizes that he must deliberately ascertain his friends' christian names in order to be able to refer to them correctly to their parents. At Oxford in the late twenties the use of the surname in these circumstances was a known *gaucherie* and must therefore have been fairly usual.[15]

p. 240. [" 'Sir' is, of course, very often used between intimates with a slightly jocular or affectionate intention; one may say 'Good morning, Sir' to almost any intimate. 'My dear Sir, I am very glad to see you.' But 'My dear Sir' usually conveys a mild remonstrance."] These usages are, I think, obsolescent among U-speakers and young U-speakers are inclined to dislike them very much. In my experience people who use them are either non-U (very often, commercial travellers) or, if U, are elderly academics.

p. 241. ["The use *'Sir'* by young men to their seniors in general is not easily defined, and the practice varies."] This is certainly true; my own use is to reserve *Sir* for men of great age and/or great distinction. The War of 1939-45, like its predecessor of 1914-18, has brought about an enormous increase in the use of *Sir* because of Service rules. Chapman says ["Young women . . . are not expected to say *sir*"]—but now many do by reason of their having been in one of the women's Services.

---

[15] In connection with surnames, I may mention a habit not noted by Chapman, viz. the abbreviation of the surnames of close friends. It was apparently U and was certainly thriving in the nineties; at a much earlier period it appears in Mrs. Henry Wood's *Johnny Ludlow* where the young *Todhetley* is often called *Tod*. The custom is now obsolescent, save perhaps in the case of hyphenated surnames (*X-Y* may be called *X*) and between close women-friends (e.g. a *Miss Robinson* might be called *Robbie*).

p. 241. ["But is there any alternative (i.e. to *Miss*) if one is addressing a telephone operator or a barmaid?"] Yes, there is: silence, perhaps the most favorite of all U-usages today. Indeed it is remarkable how easy it is (save when engaged in activities such as bridge or poker) to avoid the use of any appellation at all.[16] This has become increasingly the practice of shyer gentlemen. The use of *Miss* in the circumstances mentioned by Chapman (and particularly to waitresses) is definitely non-U.

p. 243. ["Christian names."] On this matter, Chapman has a point of view out of date even by the early thirties. I can only just remember the time, in the very early twenties, when a typical boy-and-girl conversation might have run: *"He:* May I call you by your christian name? *She:* If you like. *He:* Er—what *is* your christian name?" Since that time the use of christian names by U-speakers has been continually increasing. In the thirties, it was quite customary for a member of a *partie carée* going to a dance who was unknown to the other three to be introduced by the christian name alone (or, often, just as *John Smith* or *Jane Smith,* without prefix). In the War the use of christian names increased still further; in Government offices it was often the custom for a man at the head of a large section of girls to call them all by their christian names, while they called him *Mr. X—.*

p. 248. ["Use of surnames by women."] In the third person, it is now very usual for women to use the surname only of men (e.g. of their husbands' friends); for men, or women, to use the surnames only of women in this way is less common, though in some circles (e.g. university ones) it is quite accepted. In the second person, the use of the bare surname without christian name or prefix is rarer still. For a woman so to call a man is still either foreign, or bohemian, or intellectual-left. In general, women call other women by the bare surname only in institutions for women (e.g. in girls' schools, women's colleges, hospitals, and, no doubt, in women's prisons).

p. 250. ["Dukes: third person."] I may add that dukes, if fairly well known to the speaker, may appropriately be referred to by

---

[16] This U-habit of silence has had a curious corollary. Most nations say something when drinking (as *Skål!* in Swedish or *Egészségére!* in Hungarian) but, until 1939, English U-speakers normally said nothing. Since then, however, the Service habit of saying something has become almost universal and most U-speakers therefore feel it churlish to say nothing; repressing a shudder, they probably say *Cheers!* (though hardly *God bless!* which, though also frequent in the Services, seems non-U).

christian name and title, e.g. *George Birmingham,* meaning *George, etc., Duke of Birmingham.*

p. 251. ["A facetious use."] *His Lordship,* in facetious use, is definitely non-U and, often, inverted snob. There is a somewhat similar non-U expression: *young master* (as in *Young master's making himself quite at home!*) used of a young man considered "la-di-da" (for this word see below).

pp. 251, 255. ["Abbreviations."] *Honourable* and *Reverend* are abbreviated either as *Honble., Rev?* or as *Hon., Rev.* Both usages are quite U, though the former is the more old-fashioned.

p. 265. ["Some people say 'Miss Austen.' "] In my experience, to say *Miss Austen* instead of *Jane Austen* is either precious or pseudo-intellectual.

The Spoken Language

PRONUNCIATION   (1) In a few cases, a difference of stress serves to demarcate a pronunciation as between U and non-U. Thus *yésterdáy* (with the same stress as *Wéstern Ísles*) is non-U as against U *yésterday;* or, again, U *témporarily*/non-U *temporárily;* U *fórmidable*/non-U *formidable;* U *int'resting*/non-U *interésting; Vienna* is old-fashioned U for normal *Viénna; cónfessor* and *súccessor* (like *Mass* to rhyme with *pass,* instead of *gas*) appear to be confined to Catholic U-speakers (these call themselves *Catholic* with first syllable to rhyme with *bath*). In some cases two stress variants may both be U as *spónge cake* or *spónge cáke* (non-U-speakers hardly use the word, substituting *sponge* for it).

(2) To pronounce words like *ride* as if spelt *raid* is non-U (*raid* was, however, undoubtedly Shakespeare's pronunciation of *ride*). This kind of pronunciation is often called *refained.*

(3) Many (but not all) U-speakers make *get* rhyme with *bit, just* (adverb) with *best, catch* with *fetch.*

(4) In U speech, *spoon* rhymes with *boon,* in non-U speech with the Yorkshire pronunciation of *bun.* Some U-speakers make *gone* rhyme with *born.*

(5) U-speakers do not sound the *l* in *golf, Ralph* (which rhymes with *safe*), *solder;* some old-fashioned U-speakers do not sound it on *falcon, Malvern,* either, but it is doubtful how far this last survives.

(6) *Real, ideal* have two, respectively, three syllables in U speech, one, respectively, two in non-U speech (note, specially, non-U *really,* rhyming with *mealie*).

(7) *Fault, also, Balkans, Baltic, halt, malt, salt, vault* are pronounced by the U as if spelt *fawlt, awlso, bawlkans,* etc.

(8) In *Berkeley, Berkshire, clerk, Derby,* U-speakers rhyme the first syllable with *dark* (or *bar*), non-U speakers with *mirk* (or *burr*).[17]

(9) Some U-speakers pronounce *tire* and *tar* identically (and so for many other words, such as *fire*—even going to the length of making *lion* rhyme with *barn*).

(10) *Miscellaneous words.* (*a*) *Acknowledge:* U—rhymes with *college*/non-U—2nd syllable rhymes with *bowl*. (*b*) *Either:* U—1st syllable rhymes with *buy*/non-U—1st syllable rhymes with *bee.* (*c*) *Forehead:* U—rhymes with *torrid*/non-U—*fore-head.* (*d*) *Handkerchief:* U—last syllable rhymes with *stiff*/non-U—last syllable rhymes with *beef* or *weave.* (*e*) *Hotel and humor:* to drop the *h* is old-fashioned U. (*f*) *Medicine* and *Venison:* U—two syllables/non-U—three syllables. (*g*) U *a nought*/non-U *an ought* (meaning "zero"). (*h*) *Tortoise:* U—pronounced identically with *taught us*/non-U—last syllable rhymes with *boys* or *Boyce.* (*i*) *Vase:* U—rhymes with *bars*/ non-U—rhymes with *cause* or *maize.* (*j*) *W* (the letter):[18] U *double-you*/non-U *dubby-you.*[19]

VOCABULARY *Article* (meaning "chamber-pot") is non-U; in so far as the thing survives, U-speakers use *jerry* (a schoolboy term) or *pot.*[20]

Bath. To TAKE *a bath* is non-U against U *to* HAVE *one's bath.*

Civil: this word is used by U-speakers to approve the behavior of a non-U person in that the latter has appreciated the difference between U and non-U, e.g. *The guard was certainly very civil.*

Coach (meaning "char-à-banc") is non-U, doubtless because the

---

[17] Since it is definitely non-U to pronounce *Berkeley* with first syllable rhyming with *mirk,* U-speakers get a frisson if they have to enunciate the surnames *Birkley, Burkly* (correctly pronounced with first syllable rhyming with *mirk*) for, if a U-hearer does not appreciate the spelling of the names (rare ones), they may be suspected of using a non-U pronunciation.

[18] *The W* is a frequent non-U expression for "the lavatory" (*W. C.* is also non-U)—hence, no doubt, the non-U children's word *dubby* or *dub.* (In this connection I may mention a U expression: *Let me show you the* GEOGRAPHY *of the house* (meaning, essentially "the lavatory").)

[19] Oddly enough, *Grammar* and *Syntax* (two very important philological domains) produce hardly any marks of class-difference. I have noticed only (i) *I bought it at Woolworth* (without the final *'s*), a usage confined to some U-speakers; (ii) the non-U use of the prepositions in *He's* AT *boarding school, She's* ON *holiday;* (iii) the North Country inversion in *He's been very decent, has John.*

[20] But the (recent?) transitive verb *to pot,* used of babies, is surely non-U?

thing itself is. Those U-speakers who are forced, by penury, to use them call them *buses*, thereby causing great confusion (a *coach* runs into the country, a *bus* within a town).

non-U *corsets*/U *stays*.

Counterpane, bedspread, coverlet. Of these three synonyms, I think that the first is U, the second obsolete, the third non-U.

Cruet. The sentence *Pass the cruet, please* is very non-U; *cruets* are in themselves non-U. In gentlemen's houses there are, ideally, separate containers—*salt-cellars, pepper-pots* (*-castors, -grinders, -mills*) and *mustard-pots,* so that the corresponding U-expression will be *I wonder if you could pass the salt (pepper, mustard), please?* or the like. Vinegar is a fourth constituent of many cruets but many uses of vinegar (e.g. poured on fish or bacon-and-eggs) are definitely non-U.

Crust or crumb? used when cutting bread is (old-fashioned?) non-U.

Cultivated in *They're cultivated people* is non-U and so also is *cultured.* There is really no U-equivalent (some U-speakers use *civilized* in this sense).

Cup. How is your cup? is a non-U equivalent of *Have some more tea?* or the like. Possible negative non-U answers are *I'm doing nicely, thank you* and *(Quite) sufficient, thank you.* There is a well-known non-U affirmative answer: *I don't mind if I do* (but this was U about a century ago).

Cycle is non-U against U *bike, bicycle* (whether verb or noun); non-U *motorcycle*/U *motorbike, motorbicycle* is perhaps less pronouncedly so.

Dinner. U-speakers eat *lunch* in the middle of the day (*luncheon* is old-fashioned U) and *dinner* in the evening; if a U-speaker feels that what he is eating is a travesty of his dinner, he may appropriately call it *supper.* Non-U-speakers (also U-children and U-dogs), on the other hand, have their *dinner* in the middle of the day. *Evening meal* is non-U.

Dress-suit. This is a non-U word. A male U-speaker might answer the question *What shall I wear tonight?* in any of the following ways: (1) *Dinner jacket;* (2) *Short coat* (? old-fashioned); (3) *Black tie;* (4) *Tails;* (5) *White tie.* The term *evening dress* is often used on invitations but it has not a very wide currency among U-speakers (in any case, for men it is ambiguous); a sentence *Shall we wear evening dress?* would not be possible, the appropriate expression being *Are we going to change?*

Excuse my glove. This expression, used when shaking hands, is (? old-fashioned) non-U; male U-speakers do (used to ?) remove their glove in order to shake hands but say nothing.

Greatcoat (also *topcoat?*) are rather old-fashioned U, *overcoat* being normal. *Burberry*[21] and *raincoat* are of the same genre, *macintosh* or *mac* being normal.

Greens meaning "vegetables" is non-U.

Home: non-U *They've a lovely home*/U *They've a very nice house.*

Horse-riding is non-U against U *riding.* From the non-U point of view the expression is reasonable, for to the non-U there are other kinds of riding (cf. non-U *to go for a motor-ride*/U *to go for a drive in a motor-car*). But *bicycle-ride* is normal.

Ill in *I was very ill on the boat* is non-U against U *sick.*

Jack. At cards, *jack* is non-U against U *knave,* save in *jackpot* (at poker). My son, A. W. P. Ross, kindly calls my attention to the following passage from *Great Expectations* (ed. of 1861, vol. I, p. 126): " 'He calls the knaves, Jacks, this boy!' said Estella with disdain."

La-di-da is an expression with which the non-U stigmatize a U habit, speech-habit, or person.

Lounge is a name given by the non-U to a room in their houses; for U-speakers, *hall* or *dining-room* might well be the nearest equivalent (but all speakers, of course, speak of the *lounge* of a hotel).

non-U *mental*/U *mad.*

A matter of business is non-U (as in *Say you've come to see him on a matter of business*).

Mention: If you don't mind my mentioning it is non-U.

Mirror (save in compounds such as *driving-, shaving-mirror*) is non-U against U *looking-glass.*

non-U *note-paper*/U *writing-paper.*[22]

Pardon! is used by non-U in three main ways: (1) if the hearer does not hear the speaker properly; (2) as an apology (e.g. on brushing by someone in a passage); (3) after hiccupping or belching. The normal U-correspondences are very curt, viz. (1) *What?* (2) *Sorry!* (3) [Silence], though, in the first two cases, U-parents and U-governesses are always trying to make children say something "politer" —*What did you say?* and *I'm frightfully sorry* are certainly possible.

---

[21] This use of *Burberry* no doubt arose because, even before 1914 (when U-speakers were richer than non-U-speakers), this was a good and expensive kind of macintosh.

[22] This distinction (as well as some others, e.g. non-U *perfume*/U *scent*) is noted by Miss Nancy Mitford, *The Pursuit of Love* (1945 ed., p. 31).

For Case 3 there are other non-U possibilities, e.g. *Manners! Beg Pardon! Pardon me!*

To Pass a (nasty) remark. He passed the remark that . . . is non-U.

Pleased to meet you! This is a very frequent non-U response to the greeting *How d'you do?* U-speakers normally just repeat the greeting; to reply to the greeting (e.g. with *Quite well, thank you*) is non-U.

Posh "smart" is essentially non-U but, recently, it has gained ground among schoolboys of all classes.

non-U *preserve*/U *jam*.

non-U *radio*/U *wireless* (but *radio* technically as in aircraft).

Rude meaning "indecent" is non-U; there is no universal U-correspondent.

non-U *serviette*/U *table-napkin;* perhaps the best known of all the linguistic class-indicators of English.

Study in *He's studying for an exam.* is definitely non-U (U: *working for*).

Teacher is essentially non-U, though *school-teacher* is used by the U to indicate a non-U teacher. The U equivalent is *master, mistress* with prefixed attribute (as *maths-mistress*). Non-U children often refer to their teachers without article (as, *Teacher says . . .*).

non-U *toilet-paper*/U *lavatory-paper*.

non-U *wealthy*/U *rich*.

Before concluding with some general remarks, there are two points which may appropriately receive mention here.

First, *slang*. There seems no doubt that, in the nineties and at least up to 1914, U-speakers (particularly young ones) were rather addicted to slang. Today, however, U-speakers use it little and regard much use of it as non-U—save, of course, in special circumstances (e.g. in the case of young boys at school). American slang is especially deprecated (save, perhaps, for *O.K.*). The ultimate War, like the penultimate one, brought a flood of slang into the Services, some of it a very vivid kind as, for instance, R. A. F. slang *He tore me off a strip* meaning "he reprimanded me severely," *I was shot down in flames* meaning "I was completely overwhelmed in the argument." Since the War, there has been an unfortunate tendency for non-Service personnel to use Service slang and it is clear that Service personnel regard such use as in very poor taste. Nevertheless, the expressions *I've had it!* (meaning, essentially, "I have *not* had it") and *That's a bad show,* have become very frequent among all classes of speakers.

Secondly, *changing one's voice.*[23] In England today—just as much as in the England of many years ago—the question "Can a non-U speaker become a U-speaker?" [24] is one noticeably of paramount importance for many Englishmen (and for some of their wives). The answer is that an adult can never attain complete success. Moreover, it must be remembered that, in these matters, U-speakers have ears to hear, so that one single pronunciation, word, or phrase will suffice to brand an apparent U-speaker as originally non-U (for U-speakers themselves never make "mistakes"). Under these circumstances, efforts to change voice are surely better abandoned. But, in fact, they continue in full force and in all strata of society. On the whole, the effect is deleterious. Thus, to take only one example: in village schools, any natural dialect that is still left to the children will have superimposed upon it the language of the primary school-teacher (a class of people entirely non-U) so that the children leave school speaking a mixture which has nothing to recommend it. In concluding this paragraph, I may mention that there is one method of effecting change of voice, provided the speaker is young enough. This is, to send him[25] first to a preparatory school, then to a good public-school. This method is one that has been approved for more than a century and, at the moment, it is almost completely effective. It is interesting to speculate upon the state of affairs which will arise when the day comes when virtually no U-speaker will be able to afford to educate his children at these kinds of schools (this day has already dawned).

If we consider the wider implications of the linguistic class indication discussed above, two points immediately arise: the linguistic class indicators are almost all philologically trivial and, apparently, almost all of a very ephemeral nature. I am convinced that a thorough historical study of the class indicators discussed above would reveal many present-day U-features as non-U at an earlier period and vice versa. To take an example. In his *Critical pronouncing*

[23] This phrase is my own coinage (of many years ago); I know of no other expression.

[24] Logically, the converse question "Can a U-speaker become a non-U-speaker?" should also arise, but, in practice, it seems not to—even the staunchest of inverted snobs apparently draws the line here. At all events I have only come across one case of it (in Leeds).

[25] Today similar arrangements can be made for girls; the older approved method was, of course, a U-governess.

dictionary and expositor of the English language, published in 1791,
J. Walker is clearly trying to differentiate between U and non-U
usage. Yet nearly all the points mentioned by him—only one hundred and sixty years ago—are now "dead" and without class significance, in that one of the pronunciations given is today no longer
known in any kind of English save dialect. Only one of Walker's
U indicators (*-in'* of *huntin', shootin',* and *fishin'*) is so recognized
by me and even that one I regard as belonging to an era earlier
than my own. In two cases of double pronunciations, today's U
alternative is chosen by Walker as the non-U one, viz. (I quote)
(1) *"Either* and *neither* are . . . often pronounced *eye-ther and
nigh-ther.* . . . Analogy, however, without hesitation, gives the
dipthong the sound of long *e* and rhymes them with *breather,* one
who breathes. This is the pronunciation Mr. Garrick always gave
to these words, and which is undoubtedly the true one." (2) "The
proper names *Derby* and *Berkeley,* still retain the old sound, as if
written *Darby* and *Barkeley:* but even these, in polite usage, are
getting into the common sound, nearly as if written *Durby* and
Burkeley." Walker feels strongly on various matters: "The vulgar
. . . pronounce the *o* obscurely, and sometimes as if followed by *r,*
as *winder, feller,* for *window* and *fellow;* but this is almost too
despicable for notice"—but the pronunciation of *fellow* fulminated
against by Walker is, to me, old-fashioned U (though I make the
word rhyme with *bellow* myself).

Among European languages, English is, surely, the one most
suited to the study of linguistic class-distinction. I do not really
know how far such a thing may exist in others. In Finnish, I have
the impression that no phenomena of the sort exist. In German,
there may well have been something comparable; certainly, I recall
that, in good Potsdam society of the late twenties, the expression
küss' die hand (on introduction to a female) was definitely frowned
on—but this society has vanished without trace. In present-day Russian, the distinction between the two plurals of *ofitser* "officer"—
ofitsery and *ofitsera*—is certainly one of class. There seems to be remarkably little literature on the subject save perhaps (rather
naturally) by Russians and/or as concerns Russian. The position in
Russia is indeed interesting, for, in that country, it is obviously desirable to speak in a non-U manner rather than in a U one. (There
is an excellent book on the subject, in Russian, by Zhirmunskii.) It is
to be hoped that more studies of linguistic class-distinction in the
European languages will one day be forthcoming.

However the general concept of a certain variant of a language appertaining to a certain section of its speakers (e.g. old women, or children) is one very well known to anthropologists and it is, no doubt, in the African jungle and among the Red Indians that we shall find the generalized form of the linguistic indicators of our English class distinction. This is a suitable point at which to end this article, for we have now reached that awkward terrain where Linguistics marches with Anthropology—and the anthropologists have, alas, not been appreciably active here.

The Resources of Language

by FRIEDRICH WAISMANN

Language is always changing. That is a commonplace, yet, oddly enough, one not enough heeded by those who are clamoring for "the ordinary use of language," quite prepared, it seems, to damn everything out of hand—in philosophy—if it fails to conform to its standards. While appreciating the service done to clear thinking by the insistence on the normal use, I feel that the time has come to say a word of warning against the cult of it, for such it has almost become. Like any cult, while it is likely to protect its votaries from certain dangers—getting trapped in the vagaries of speech— it is apt to make them blind to the obvious narrowness of such a view, particularly when it is just on the point of becoming one of the major influences of our time. It tends to instil, in the faithful and in the not-so-faithful alike, a belief, a complacent one, in the adequacy of language which is far from the truth. In actual fact, language is a deficient instrument, and treacherous in many ways. As this opens a subject of vast dimensions I shall confine myself to a few scattered observations.

First, I shall try to argue that a departure from the beaten track need not only not be anathematized, but may be the *very thing* to be strived for—in poetry, science and in philosophy. My second point is that language, far from serving merely to report facts, is a collective instrument of thought that enters experience itself, shaping and molding the whole apprehension of phenomena (such as color and luster, e.g.) in a certain definite way, and, who knows, giving to them just that subtle bias which makes all the difference. How curiously different, for instance, must the world of color have appeared to the Romans who had in their language no word for gray, brown, nor any *generic* word for blue (though they had a number of words to denote particular shades of this color). How curiously different, it would seem, must human action appear when seen through the filter of Eskimo language where, owing to the lack of transitive verbs, it is likely to be perceived as a sort of happening without an active element in it. (In Greenlandic one cannot say "I kill him," "I shoot the arrow," but only "He dies to me," "The arrow is flying away from me," just as "I hear" is expressed by "me-sound-is.") Eskimo philosophers, if there were any, would be likely to say that what we call action is "really" a pattern, or gestalt, of succeeding impressions. Just as Greenlandic assimilates action to impression—which strikes us as strange—so our language tends to bias us in just the opposite way: it makes us assimilate perception to action. We say not only "I cut the tree," but also "I see the tree": the use of the same construction makes it appear as if the "I" was the *subject* from which issued the seeing, and as if the seeing was a sort of action directed at the tree; nor are we any better off if we use the passive voice "The tree is seen by me"—for now it almost looks as if something *happened* to the tree, as if it had to undergo or suffer my seeing it. Following the clues of speech, we are led to interpret the world of experience one-sidedly, just as "owing to the common philosophy of grammar," as Nietzsche put it, i.e. "owing to the unconscious domination and guidance of similar grammatical functions the way seems barred against certain other possibilities of world-interpretation." In other words, every language contains, deep-sunken in it, certain molds, designs, forms to apprehend phenomena, human action, etc. It is hardly going too far to say that a whole world picture is wedded to the use of the transitive verb and the actor-action scheme that goes with it—that if we spoke a different language we would perceive a different world. By growing up in a certain language, by thinking in its semantic and syntactical grooves, we acquire a certain more or less uniform outlook on the world—an outlook we are scarcely aware of until (say) by coming across a language of a totally different structure we are shocked into seeing the oddity of the obvious, or what seemed to be obvious. Finally, I want to say that philosophy *begins* with distrusting language—that medium that pervades, and warps, our very thought. But this is perhaps too strong an expression. I do not mean to say that language *falsifies* experience, twists it into something else; the point is that it supplies us with certain categorical forms without which the formation of a coherent system of experience, a world picture, would be impossible. In this sense, language shapes and fashions the frame in which experience is set, and different languages achieve this in different ways. A philosopher, more than others, should be sensitive to this sort of influence, alive to the dangers that lie dormant in the forms of expression—the very thing, that is, which, so misguidedly, has been raised to the standard in philosophical controversy.

When I spoke of the change of language I was not thinking of those cases which delight the heart of a philologist—umlaut, ablaut, and the like. Nor was I referring to changes in meaning and vocabulary—what was originally stupid, wanton, Latin *nescius,* becomes "nice"; a horse that is well fed and grows a smooth, shiny coat is "glad"—*glatt* in German; what is now silly was formerly "sely" corresponding to German *selig*—happy, blessed; for while such changes are instructive in many ways, they are hardly such as to deserve the philosopher's attention. Neither was I thinking of those more subtle changes in the *valeurs* for a word which—as in the case of "romantic"—are significant of a change in the tone of thought of a whole period—of a half-conscious awakening of new ways of feeling and responses to nature, so elusive and yet, to the historian, so important. What I had in mind were cases which are best illustrated by a few examples.

Nothing is so opposed as day and night; yet there is a sense, as when we speak of a "three days' journey," in which "day" includes night. "Man" is used in contrast to woman, but occasionally as a term including woman; and a similar shift of sense is perceptible in "he" and "she"—as an arguer, also woman is "he." We say of a child that he is two years "old," not two years "young," just as we inquire "How *long* (not how *short*) will you stay?" or "How *far* (not how *near*) is it from here to the station?" The word "quality," while for the most part used indifferently, is sometimes uttered in a peculiar tone—as when we say "He has quality." White and black are commonly contrasted with colors in the strict and proper sense ("illustrations in color" *versus* "illustrations in black and white"), yet in certain contexts we are inclined to reckon them amongst the colors; as when we say "Look round you—everything you see has some color or other," thinking, perhaps, that even air and vapor, or glass and water are possessed by some very pale, some very pearly tone. Thus "color" tends to absorb into its meaning all shades, even black and white, the otherwise "colorless" hues. But these are instances betraying a deeper drift. In the ordinary sense, motion is opposed to rest, speed to slowness, size to littleness, numerous to a few, depth to shallowness, strength to weakness, value to worthlessness, just as far is opposed to near, hot to cold, dry to wet, dark to bright, heavy to light, and true to false. And this was, roughly, the way in which Greek philosophers regarded such contrasts. "Up" for them was simply "not-down," "soft" "not-hard," "dry" "not wet," and so on.[1] The fact that two polar terms were in use may have played a role in underpinning the belief that things which are hot and cold, or hard and soft, etc., are different, not in degree, but in kind—a fateful belief, for on it hinged their under-standing—no, their lack of understanding of change. They signally failed to penetrate it. The Greeks never mastered the problem of motion—which is but the simplest case—they never evolved a science of dynamics, which is surprising enough in view of their genius for mathematics. They give the impression that they somehow got started on the wrong track—for them heavenly and terrestrial mo-tion were entirely different, the one governed by law, eternal and unchanging, the other lawless, corrupt, confused; if faced with a change, such as a thing getting heated, they thought that one quality must be destroyed to let the opposite quality take its place. Thus they were, perhaps as a consequence of their quaint ideas, mightily impeded in coming to grips with the problem of change.

In science a language has come into use in which those contrasted terms are looked upon as degrees of one and the same quality— darkness as light intensity of illumination, slowness as the lower range of speed, rest as the limiting case of motion; there is a scale only of hardness, not of softness, only a physical theory of heat, not a theory of coldness; what we measure is the strength of a rope, a current, etc., not its weakness, what we count is number, not few-ness; the air has a degree of moisture, not of dryness; and everything has weight and mass, even an electron. Again, we speak of health irrespective of whether it is good or bad health, and of the value of things which are of no value. Under the influence of such exam-ples, it would seem, a term like "truth-value" has been coined to cover both truth and falsity of a statement, just as "verification" is, prevalently, used to include falsification. "Distance," "width," "wealth," "intelligence" are further nouns which had the same career; though the same is not so true of the adjectives—"distant," "wealthy," "intelligent" are not yet relativized, any more than "hard," "hot," "speedy," "weighty" are, or "healthy," "valuable" and "worthy"; on the contrary, they retain the original sense. Ad-jectives, it would appear, have a much tougher life than nouns, and not only in English. But that only in passing.

Here we see a whole array of terms shifting in a parallel way, and

[1] See e.g. A. P. Rossiter, *The Growth of Science* (New York: Pitman Publishing Corp., 1939).

in a way which is of far-reaching consequence: for the construction of modern science is bound up with it and would not have been possible without it. The changeover from the static view—where the adjective is seen as the expression of a permanent quality—to a dynamic which apprehends quality as a variable degree within a certain scale made possible "functional thinking" (I use the word as mathematicians do), the kind of thinking that can cope with change and the conceptual difficulties it presents. What happened was obviously this: one term of a pair of contraries had a tendency to swallow up the other and stand for the whole range of variation. Whether this tendency can be traced to the rationalizing influence of science, or whether it is prior to science and has itself given an impetus to that revolution of thought is a question still undecided.[2] It is in this context, perhaps, not without significance that Latin and Greek were lacking in all the finer means to express continuous change and functional dependence: in Latin, for instance, there are no *general* terms to express the relation "the more—the less"; the phrases used for "the more—the more" are confined to simple *proportionality*, the analogue to *statics*.[3] Nor has any classical language an equivalent for "to become" (*devenir* in French, *devenire* in medieval Latin) so essential to our way of describing a change in quality, for neither *fieri* nor γίγνεσθαι can be used in the same way to express the idea of *continuous* change. There are no uses of intransitive verbs such as "to soften," (*rubesco* is inceptive), etc.

The new idiom, which sprang up first in the vernacular about the 14th century, has not entirely displaced the older one (as can still be seen from the adjectives cited above). Both exist side by side. Though the use of "moisture" for dry as well as wet (as in meteorology), or of "truth-value" in logic still has the ring of jargon, in other instances the new idiom has become completely naturalised —as with "distance" for near and far, "age" for young and old, "size" for big and small "density" for thick and thin. Yet even so, we can use any such term in two distinct ways—we may ask *"Is* he old?" or *"How* old is he?"; and so in the other cases.

At the time of Nicole Oresme, Bishop of Lisieux, when a new way of looking at change was growing up, and with it a new way of speaking of qualities, this must have been felt as a shocking de-

---

[2] My attention has been drawn to this aspect of the matter by my former pupil J. L. Hevesi.

[3] Cf. Karl Ettmayer, Ritter von, *Analytische Syntax der französischen Sprache* (Halle: N. Niemeyer, 1936), II, 935 ff.

parture from the ordinary use, supported and sanctioned as it was by old tradition. How the cloisters of the schoolmen must have resounded with "intensio et remissio formarum"—the disputes as to whether a quality might have degrees and, in changing, could yet remain the same, or whether this was patent nonsense. One may imagine the indignant outcries of the purists of the time, their loathing of what must have appeared to them as "new-fangled ways of speaking" and as a "complete perversion" of grammar. The latter, more even than the vocabulary, embodies a good deal of the conservatism of mankind, and progress had often to be made in the teeth of the enormous resistance offered by its structure to ways of thinking which do not, or not smoothly, fit its grooves. (See what has been said in the foregoing on Greek language and absence of dynamics.) Grammar draws a *cordon sanitaire* against any rebellious ideas that dare to crop up.

The importance of functional correlation can, moreover, be seen in a different domain: in perspective, and the enthusiasm with which it was universally greeted when it was discovered—another coincidence?—at the very time when new aspects of thought and feeling were just about to take shape: Duccio's Maesta and Giotto's wall paintings in the Capella degli Scrovegni in Padua both belong to the early 14th century. The "strange fascination which perspective had for the Renaissance mind cannot be accounted for exclusively by a craving for verisimilitude," as Panofsky[4] observes. A sensibility to functional relation is apparent in this, and the interest in perspective—so alien to the Greeks—is almost symbolic of the time. A reflex of it can still be caught from the writings of Leonardo da Vinci and Dürer. As perspective rests essentially on a clear understanding of the way in which two variables, the apparent size of an object and its distance from the beholder, are connected, Leonardo saw in painting a "science." He certainly must have been struck by the affinity between this "science" and the philosophical speculations on dynamics of the schoolmen of which he was fully aware (he even employed their ideas in his theory of painting).

If those pedantic schoolmen and -masters had had their way, there would today be no science and no dynamics; but, for consolation, "correct" grammar. To look at any departure from the norm as a crime is nothing but a blind prejudice; and a fateful one at that as it tends to drain the life-blood of any independent inquiry. Lan-

[4] E. Panofsky, *Albrecht Dürer* (Princeton, N. J.: Princeton University Press, 1945), I, 260.

guage is an instrument that must as occasion requires, be bent to one's purpose. To stick to language as it is can only lead to a sort of Philistinism which insists on the observance of the cliché and will end up with a harakiri of living thought. Indeed, the guardian of language who jealously watches over its "correctness" is in the long run bound to turn into a reactionary who looks askance at any innovation. Correctness is a useful, but a negative virtue. Follow those prophets, and you will soon find yourself imprisoned in a language cage, clean, disinfected, and unpleasant like a sanatorium room.

Understandably enough, there is an instinctive prejudice against neologisms, in part springing from a wholesome fear that novelty of speech may screen poverty of thought. We all dislike new words. And yet there is another and perfectly proper urge to give expression to meanings so far unexpressed, or, in the present language, indeed inexpressible. When Freud, for instance, says *der Patient erinnert den Vorfall* he is using the verb *erinnern* in a novel manner; in the ordinary way, the verb is used reflexively, *sich an etwas erinnern*. Why has Freud (who wrote a very good style) diverged at this point? There is a queer way in which a neurotic person who is under treatment may suddenly remember long-forgotten scenes of his early life which, as Freud puts it, have been "repressed" and are now being relived. What has been inaccessible to the patient, however hard he may have tried, breaks, in a violent storm of emotion, through to consciousness. In order to set apart this kind of remembrance from the ordinary one where we remember at will, Freud uses the verb transitively, in a way no one has done before; and with this syntactical innovation goes a semantic change. By this use Freud has enriched the German language. Such stray deviations, hit upon in a lucky hour and accepted by custom, these little, yet expressive departures from the beaten track, have not only a vividness, a sparkle of their own, but they sharpen the tools of thought and keep language from going blunt. So why cavil at them?

What those sticklers for correctness prefer not to see is that we are living in a *changing world,* and that language is always lagging behind these changes. To cite only one sort of examples out of a great many parallel ones—in psychological experiments one constantly comes across situations which call for new ways of describing. If Maxwell disks, for instance, are rotated one sees, so long as the movement is slow, several color sectors, and when the disk is spinning rapidly, a uniform color, the result of fusion, but in between there is a certain point where a flicker is seen. There are cases in which the color itself is seen flickering, and others, as when the disk is watched through a small screen-hole, which are more aptly described by saying that there is a flickering *across* the disk or *before* it in space, or again that the disk's surface is seen *behind* the flicker. These modes of expression, though perfectly natural and instantly understood by every one, yet digress from the norm. For "before" and "behind," while clearly denoting spatial relations, are used in such a way that it makes no longer sense to ask, "Exactly how many millimeters before the disk is the flickering?" Here we have a sense of "before" which admits of no distance. To cite a few similar cases —if we look at a metal its color seems to lie *behind* its surface, just as its glitter appears *in front of,* or *superimposed* on it; the glow of a piece of red-hot iron is seen not simply as color that lies on its surface but as *extending* back into the object. Again, it has been said that, when a person is speaking with someone in complete darkness, the voice of the other sounds distinctly *behind* the darkness, not *in* the darkness. In some cases an object is seen as "desurfaced," with a filmy, fluffy sort of outline, a bit unreal perhaps. Queer idioms which say what cannot quite be said by anything else: but condemn them on account of that? Notice with what unerring instinct language contrives to say, at the cost of a slight departure, what would be unsayable if we moved along the rigid grooves of speech. Indeed, how should one describe such phenomena if not by breaking away from the clichés? Is there anything objectionable in that? If so, language could never keep pace with life. Yet new situations, unforseen, arise, and with them the need of describing them; it can only be met by adjusting language—either by coining new words, or, as the word-creating faculty is scanty, by pressing old ones into new services, in this way cutting through the dead mass of convention. It is precisely because speech runs so much in ready-made molds that an occasional anomaly, a happy flouting of the laws of grammar, an uncommon phrasing, arouses our attention and lends luster to the point we want to bring out. It is in this way, by *transgressing,* that language manages to achieve what it is meant to achieve, and that it grows. Why, then, the squeamishness?

Not only should the scientist be free to deviate from common language, where the need arises, but he is bound to do so if he is to convey a new insight not in conformity with the ideas dominant of the time, with ideas, moreover, precipitated in language. The classical example of this is Einstein. When he was groping his way, there was, in his own words, "a feeling of direction," of going towards something he didn't quite know—which centered more and more on a suspicion that all was not well with the idea of simultaneity. He could at first not say what was wrong with it, and yet felt that here, if anywhere, was the key to all the dark puzzles that troubled the physicists at that time. Had he been brought up as a pupil of G. E. Moore, imbued with a belief in the infallibility of the ordinary modes of expression, he could never have made his discovery, clogged as he would have been by the dead weight of usage. As it was, he paid no respect to common sense, let alone the common speech. He insisted on asking himself, Do I *really* understand what I mean when I say that two events are simultaneous? Once the question was brought into sharp focus, he came to see, gradually perhaps and to his surprise, that there was a gap in his understanding. For the sense in which we speak of two events happening at the same time, when they are in the same place, or nearby, cannot be applied to events in distant places. It would be *blind*, he felt, to apply the familiar meaning of "simultaneous" to these other cases—it would only land us in perplexities beyond resolve. Einstein saw that the term "simultaneous" had first to be *defined* for the case of distant events, and defined in such a way that the definition supplies us with a method to decide experimentally whether or not two events are simultaneous. This "seeing" of a crucial point in the meaning of "simultaneous" has *absolutely* nothing to do with the way the word is actually used in language. It is as well to remind you that in 1905, when Einstein's first essay appeared, there was only *one* use, not two uses of "simultaneous," and that it would be absurd to pretend that, when Einstein found a difference in meaning, he was making a *linguistic* discovery. (A sidelight on how wrong the philosophical equation meaning = is.) On the contrary, anyone who had taken ordinary language, or common sense, for his guide, and had been asked whether he understood what "simultaneous" meant, would have replied with a decided Yes—no matter whether he could, or could not, specify a method for finding out. He would have said that the meaning of the word is clear in itself and needs no further explanation. In fact, no one before Einstein, whether a plain man, a scientist, or a philosopher, doubted for a minute that the concept was clear to him, so clear that he need not trouble. That's precisely what made people slur over the decisive point. Einstein *saw*: that is how he freed himself from the thought-habits imposed on us by speech, radically so. By following the lead of language, or of the common sense philosophers one would have barred oneself from the spark of insight which was to be the dawn of a new era in physics.

These facts speak for themselves. That science cannot live under the tutelage of any ideas on "correctness," will perhaps be conceded.

But this is true not only of science. Poetry is forever groping along the borders of the unspeakable, wresting new land from the vast void of the unexpressed. It is its mission to break through the wall of conventional views that encloses us, to startle us into seeing the world through fresh eyes. This is what all the great poets from Dante to Baudelaire have performed, and that is their glory. However, it is a large subject, too large to be treated here. I shall pick out only one tiny point, and one, moreover, that concerns prose— Flaubert's style which, in Proust's phrase, has "renewed our vision of things." In a work of fiction, nature is usually treated as background to men; against this background stand out the main characters of the story, the way they act, think, speak, feel and behave. The contrast between the uniformity of nature and the uniqueness of the human world is, in French, expressed by the use of two tenses —the imperfect for things and processes, and the perfect for men and actions. But with Flaubert, what men do is, in essence, always the same—it is like the succession of rain and sunshine, spring and summer, the ripening of the corn, and the phases of the moon. There is something dull and repetitive about them which pervades them with a sort of dispassionate sadness. There is a passage in *Madame Bovary* where Flaubert speaks of "the eternal monotony of passion which has ever the same forms and the same language." A revealing passage; for what he has tried to do and has done is to bring about something like a shift in our way of seeing people and things; and this he achieves, simply, by his relentless use of the imperfect, assimilating, in language, his apprehension of men to that of things (remember Greenlandic!). Everything, including human action, is resolved into a perpetual and monotonous flux, revealing the melancholy essence of human existence. Describing people in the forms appropriate to things produces a peculiar effect indeed—"what, up to the time of Flaubert, had been merely action, has become impression," as Proust puts it. As we read over the pages of his novels, we are made to feel in what people say that they would always say precisely the same thing, that their whole life can be poured into a phrase as into a little vial. And when the perfect is used—on rare occasions only as when the narrative changes direction—it is again with a queer effect: it gives to a thing (when it occupies the place of a subject) a character of activity, it is as if a furtive ray of sunlight was falling on it, imparting to it, for a fleeting instant, a life of its own: change suddenly turns into action. And from this arises that unique Flaubertian vision of things which, like any artist's vision, can only be communicated through his style. Besides the tenses, the conjunction "and" is used in an entirely new way. It hardly ever binds phrase to phrase, but has a more musical function —to mark a pause in the beat of the rhythm, to indicate that the moving wave we have been following has spent itself, and that another is about to build itself up. To this must be added a novel use of the present participles, of adverbs, and of certain pronouns and prepositions—grammatical peculiarities which all contribute to give shape to a world picture in which life is seen as a smooth change of one state passing into another without the persons taking any active part in the action—a picture that reminds one of some huge escalator which goes on and on, never stopping, never breaking its monotony. But where an "action" does intervene in the flow of events, its protagonists are, in general, *things,* acting on a plane of nonhuman drama. What a vision! And yet a vision attained by distorting syntax. This, I think, should be enough to instil a drop of scepticism into the belief that all is well with ordinary language; it makes one wonder whether there is not, after all, a hard atom of truth in the view that ordinary speech is only good for saying things that are no longer worth saying.

By giving so copious examples my aim was to drive home the point defended here—that the ideal of correctness is a deadening one, that it is in vain to set up a language police to stem living developments. (I have always suspected that correctness is the last refuge of those who have nothing to say.)

Poets and literary critics feel, today perhaps more keenly than ever before, that there is something disquieting about language. If I correctly read the signs, there is a susceptibility to the perils of words, a growing one, and a suspicion that language comes between us and the things we want to say. "In speaking one always says more than one intends to" observes Sartre; and T. S. Eliot, having noticed the vanity of words to express what is unique in experience, says "The particular has no language." Philosophers, on the other hand, are on the whole more likely to be found in the opposite camp— "debunking" all this talk as "pseudo-complaints which masquerade as genuine." [5] I think that this is a mistaken attitude for a number of reasons, and this is perhaps the place to set out some of them.

First, to talk of *the* ordinary use of language is, as I have already hinted in a previous article, unrealistic. Though I would not go so far as Ezra Pound in saying that our whole speech is "churning and

[5] Alice Ambrose, "The Problems of Linguistic Inadequacy," *Philosophical Analysis,* ed. Max Black (Ithaca, N. Y.: Cornell University Press, 1950).

chugging" today, the fact remains that language is in a state of flux. But, it will be said, that is the concern of the historian of language, not of the philosopher. All the philosopher needs to know is the *stock* use of a word or phrase, as it is employed at present, in contrast with its nonstock uses.[6] This answer is unsatisfactory. Though it would be silly to pretend that one did not know the stock use of "cat" or "shut the door," there are other cases where one would feel less sure. Is a "taste of onions" the stock use and a "taste for history" derived, secondary, figurative? (But it is not *felt* as a metaphor!) Is only a "brilliant sunshine" standard use and a "brilliant style" nonstandard? Is "day" as opposed to night, or as including night the norm? What about speaking of a "wild laughter," a "brooding silence," or saying that a "recollection of this experience moved in his eyes"? It is easy to see that the "stock use" shifts with the context, and shifts in time. What was stock use may become obsolescent and fall into the limbo of silence, just as new uses may spring up and may, in their turn, become standard language; but where is one to draw the line? It is well to remember that almost all expressions which refer to the mental are derived from others whose primary sense was sensuous and that this is a process which goes on to the present day; just as a good many words, under the influence of science, philosophy, or something still more elusive, have only in fairly recent times undergone a change in meaning—e.g. "organic," "nervous," "unconscious," "original," "creative," "objective," "curiosity," "to entail," etc. There is continuous change and continuous creation in language. Finally, there is such a thing as ambiguity which—except in exceptional cases—mars any attempt to single out one use as the stock one. Exactly how many standard uses has "nature"? What about "in," "on," "about" etc.? "The English prepositions," says Empson, "from being used in so many ways and in combination with so many verbs, have acquired not so much a number of meanings as a body of meaning continuous in several dimensions."[7] If so, or if the uses shade off into one another imperceptibly, how can one peel off and throw away all the nonstock uses and retain the stock ones? Yes, this view *is* unrealistic.

Next, and this raises a bigger issue, even if there was such a thing as a stock use, it need not matter much to the philosopher. I mean, he need not be *bound* to this use; I should even go further and say

[6] I am indebted here to Prof. G. Ryle for letting me read an article of his in which such distinctions are discussed.

[7] William Empson, *Seven Types of Ambiguity* (New York: Harcourt, Brace & World, Inc., 1931), p. 5.

that, sooner or later, he is bound to commit the crime and depart from it—that is, if he has something new to say. In this respect, his position is not altogether different from that of the poet or the scientist, and for similar reasons. He, too, may have come to see something which, in the ordinary way, cannot quite be said. I shall argue later that this is a characteristic feature of some philosophising. To mention here just one small point, the English language has been enriched by many words coined by philosophers who were sensitive to gaps in our vocabulary. "Optimism," for instance, is due to Leibniz, and was borrowed from him by Voltaire. "Impression" in its modern sense was introduced by Hume, "intuition" by De Quincey, "intuitionism" by Sidgwick, "intuitionist" by H. Spencer. "Scientist" is an invention of Whewell, "aesthetic" one of Baumgarten, and so on. That even the laws of grammar can be flouted with salubrious effect can be seen from Lichtenberg's remark that one should say "It thinks in me."

My third point is that certain features of one's own language are noticed and appreciated in their full significance only when it is compared with other languages—with German (verbal way of expressing color), Greenlandic (dominance of the impression verb), Latin (absence of words for blue, grey, and brown), etc. Is, then, the philosopher to go to the Eskimos to learn his trade? Not exactly; yet the mere *awareness* of other possibilities is, philosophically, of the utmost importance: it makes us see in a flash other ways of world interpretation of which we are unaware, and thus drives home what is conventional in our outlook. The technique of the ordinary-use philosophers has suffered from the fact that they restricted themselves to the study of one language to the exclusion of any other— with the result that they became blind to those ubiquitous features of their own language on which their whole mode of thinking, indeed their world picture, depends.

Connected with this is another large point—the misleadingness of our speech forms. That language, "the embodied and articulated Spirit of the Race," as Coleridge put it, is in many ways inadequate can, I take it, by no one be doubted. In particular, it is the syntax and the field of analogies embedded in language which, unperceived, hold our thought in thrall, or push it along perilous lines. We shall soon have occasion to substantiate this point.

But there are still more reasons for guarding against this official doctrine. The one is that its champions pay heed only to the actual use of language not to its gaps revealing as they are. Suppose, for instance, that I say "I ought to do so-and-so"; when I say that it is obvious that the I is here only a pseudo-subject from which the ought seems to proceed, whereas in fact it is more a *point d'appui* to which it is directed. We regard a rule of ethics, politeness, etc., as something outside ourselves which applies to us as objects. We are rather in a passive (obedient) frame of mind, and what is active is, at most, the consent we give to that duty. "I am under an obligation," "it is my duty" are therefore phrases which are more appropriate. That "ought" does not refer to an occult activity betrays itself in a number of features; thus we do not say "I will ought," "I choose (decide) to ought," any more than we say "I ought to ought," or "I am resolved upon oughting." There is no such thing as a "will to ought." The complete absence of these idioms *is* revealing. That philosophers have concentrated on the use, and neglected the nonuse of expressions is a further weakness of their technique.

Essentially Contested Concepts

by W. B. GALLIE

Introductory

Any particular use of any concept of common sense or of the natural sciences is liable to be contested for reasons better or worse; but whatever the strength of the reasons they usually carry with them an assumption of agreement, as to the *kind* of use that is appropriate to the concept in question, between its user and anyone who contests his particular use of it. When this assumption cannot be made, we have a widely recognized ground for philosophical inquiry. Thus, "This picture is painted in oils" may be contested on the ground that it is painted in tempera, with the natural assumption that the disputants agree as to the proper use of the terms involved. But "This picture is a work of art" is liable to be contested because of an evident disagreement as to—and the consequent need for philosophical elucidation of—the proper general use of the term "work of art."

What forms could the required elucidation take? The history of philosophy suggests three. A philosopher might in some way discover, and persuade others that he had discovered, a meaning of the hitherto contested concept to which all could henceforward agree. Alternatively, a philosopher might propose a meaning for the contested term to which, rather than continue in their previous disagreement, the disputants might decide henceforward to conform. Thirdly, he might claim to prove or explain the necessity (relative to certain explanatory conditions) of the contested character of the concept in question, as for instance Kant tried to do in his Antinomies. Recently, however, we have been taught that effective philosophical elucidations are likely to be of a much more complicated and elusive character than any of the above, and there is today a widespread repudiation of the idea of philosophy as a kind of "engine" of thought, that can be laid on to eliminate conceptual confusions wherever they may arise. Now without wishing to advocate a return to any extreme form of this latter view, I hope to show, in the case of an important group of concepts, how acceptance of a single method of approach—of a single explanatory hypothesis calling for some fairly rigid schematization—*can* give us enlightenment of a much needed kind.

The concepts which I propose to examine relate to a number of organized or semi-organized human activities: in academic terms they belong to aesthetics, to political philosophy, to the philosophy of history and the philosophy of religion. My main thought with regard to them is this. We find groups of people disagreeing about the proper use of the concepts, e.g., of art, of democracy, of the Christian tradition. When we examine the different uses of these terms and the characteristic arguments in which they figure we soon see that there is no one clearly definable general use of any of them which can be set up as the correct or standard use. Different uses of the term "work of art" or "democracy" or "Christian doctrine" subserve different though of course not altogether unrelated functions for different schools or movements of artists and critics, for different political groups and parties, for different religious communities and sects. Now once this *variety* of functions is disclosed it might well be expected that the disputes in which the above mentioned concepts figure would at once come to an end. But in fact this does not happen. Each party continues to maintain that the special functions which the term "work of art" or "democracy" or "Christian doctrine" fulfills on *its* behalf or on *its* interpretation, is the correct or proper or primary, or the only important, function which the term in question can plainly be said to fulfill. Moreover, each party continues to defend its case with what it claims to be convincing arguments, evidence and other forms of justification.

When this kind of situation persists in practical life we are usually wise to regard it as a head-on conflict of interests or tastes or attitudes, which no amount of discussion can possibly dispel; we are consequently inclined to dismiss the so-called rational defences of the contesting parties as at best unconscious rationalizations and at worst sophistical special pleadings. On the other hand, when this kind of situation persists in philosophy (where some disputant continues to maintain against all comers that there is one and only one proper sense of the term "substance" or "self" or "idea") we are inclined to attribute it to some deep-seated and profoundly interesting

intellectual tendency, whose presence is "metaphysical"—something
to be exorcized with skill or observed with fascination according to
our philosophical temperament. Now I have no wish to deny that
endless disputes may be due to psychological causes on the one hand
or to metaphysical afflictions on the other; but I want to show that
there are apparently endless disputes for which neither of these explanations *need* be the correct one. Further, I shall try to show that
there are disputes, centered on the concepts which I have just mentioned, which are perfectly genuine: which, although not resolvable
by argument of any kind, are nevertheless sustained by perfectly
respectable arguments and evidence. This is what I mean by saying
that there are concepts which are essentially contested, concepts the
proper use of which inevitably involves endless disputes about their
proper uses on the part of their users.

I shall first set out in some detail a highly artificial example of
an essentially contested concept, with a view to showing how any
proper use of this concept is in the nature of the case contestable,
and will, as a rule, be actually contested by and in another use of it,
which in the nature of the case is contestable, and will . . . and so
on for an indefinite number of kinds of possible use: these mutually
contesting, mutually contested uses of the concept, making up together its standard general use. Then I shall list, with a view to
logical "placing" of this kind of concept, a number of semi-formal
conditions to which any concept of this kind must conform, and
shall indicate the different relations of these conditions to any such
concept, again making use of my artificial example. I shall then discuss some live examples which approximate closely to my artificial
example, so that, despite their several peculiarities, I think I can
reasonably be said to have explained or justified their use by comparing them with it. I shall next discuss what seem to me the most
important implications of my new grouping of concepts for general
philosophy, and shall conclude by trying to meet some objections
that might naturally be raised against it.

The Artificial Example

We are all acquainted with the concept of "championship" or of
"the champions" in various games and sports. Commonly a team is
judged or agreed to be "the champions" at regular intervals, e.g.,
annually, in virtue of certain features of its performance against
other contesting teams. Then for a certain period, e.g., a year, this
team is by definition "the champions" even though, as months go

by, it becomes probable or certain that they will not repeat their success. But now let us imagine a championship of the following kind. (I) In this championship each team specializes in a distinctive method, strategy and style of play of its own, to which all its members subscribe to the best of their ability. (II) "Championship" is not adjudged and awarded in terms of the highest number of markable successes, e.g., "scores," but in virtue of level of style or calibre. (No doubt for this to be manifested a certain minimum number of successes is necessary.) More simply, to be adjudged "the champions" means to be judged "to have played the game best." (III) "Championship" is not a distinction gained and acknowledged at a fixed time and for a fixed period. Games proceed continuously, and whatever side is acknowledged champion today knows it may perfectly well be caught up or surpassed tomorrow. (IV) Just as there is no "marking" or "points" system to decide who are the champions, so there are no official judges or strict rules of adjudication. Instead what happens is this. Each side has its own loyal kernel group of supporters, and in addition, at any given time, a number of "floating" supporters who are won over to support it because of the quality of its play—and, we might add, the loudness of its kernel supporters' applause and the persuasiveness of their comments. Moreover, at any given time, *one* side will have the largest (and loudest) group of supporters who, we may say, will *effectively* hail it as "the champions." But (V) the supporters of *every* contesting team regard and refer to their favored team as "the champions" (perhaps allowing such qualifications as "the *true* champions," "the *destined* champions," "*morally* the champions" . . . and so on). To bring out the importance of this point, we may suppose that all groups of supporters would acknowledge that at a given moment one team T_1 are "the effective champions." Yet the property of being acknowledged effective champions carries with it no universal recognition of outstanding excellence—in T_1's style and calibre of play. On the contrary, the supporters of T_2, T_3, etc., continue to regard and to acclaim their favored teams as "the champions" and continue with their efforts to convert others to their view, not through any vulgar wish to be the majority party, but because they believe their favored team is *playing the game best*. There is, therefore, continuous competition between the contestant teams, not only for acknowledgement as champions, but for acceptance of (what each side and its supporters take to be) the proper criteria of championship.

The Conditions of Essential Contestedness

In order to count as essentially contested, in the sense just illustrated, a concept must possess the four following characteristics: (1) it must be *appraisive* in the sense that it signifies or accredits some kind of valued achievement. (2) This achievement must be of an internally complex character, for all that its worth is attributed to it as a whole. (3) Any explanation of its worth must therefore include reference to the respective contributions of its various parts or features; yet prior to experimentation there is nothing absurd or contradictory in any one of a number of possible rival descriptions of its total worth, one such description setting its component parts or features in one order of importance, a second setting them in a second order, and so on. In fine, the accredited achievement is *initially* variously describable. (4) The accredited achievement must be of a kind that admits of considerable modification in the light of changing circumstances; and such modification cannot be prescribed or predicted in advance. For convenience I shall call the concept of any such achievement "open" in character.[1]

There seem to me to be the four most important necessary conditions to which any essentially contested concept must comply. But they do not define what it is to be a concept of this kind. For this purpose we should have to say not only that different persons or parties adhere to different views of the correct use of some concept but (5) that each party recognizes the fact that its own use of it is contested by those of other parties, and that each party must have at least some appreciation of the different criteria in the light of which the other parties claim to be applying the concept in question. More simply, to use an essentially contested concept means to use it against other uses and to recognize that one's own use of it has to be maintained against these other uses. Still more simply, to use an essentially contested concept means to use it both aggressively and defensively.

[1] We might rewrite conditions (3) and (4) above as follows: (3a) Any essentially contested concept is liable initially to be *ambiguous*, since a given individual P_1 may apply it having in mind description D_1 of the achievement which the concept accredits, and his application of it may be accepted (or rejected) by other people who have in mind different descriptions, D_2, D_3, etc., of the accredited achievement. But this *initial* ambiguity must be considered in conjunction with condition (5) below. (4a) Any essentially contested concept is *persistently* vague, since a proper use of it by P_1 in a situation S_1 affords no sure guide to anyone else as to P_1's next, and perhaps equally proper, use of it in some future situation S_2.

I will now discuss these five conditions in terms of my artificial example. There can be no question but that my concept of "the champions" is appraisive; nor, I think, that it is used both aggressively and defensively. This disposes of conditions (1) and (5). What of condition (2) that the achievement of championship (by playing the game best) must be of an internally complex character? Are all worthwhile achievements essentially internally complex? That they are seems to me as certain as any statement about values and valuation can be; and although I admit that there is plenty to be said and asked about why this is so, I don't think it necessary to embark on such discussion here. To meet condition (3)—the variously describable character of the achievement which the term "the champions" accredits—we may imagine that our championship is to be gained by playing a game something like skittles. The only action it demands from all members of any contesting side is a kind of bowling at certain objects. But such bowling can be judged, from the point of view of method, strategy, and style, in a number of different ways: particular importance may be attached to speed or to direction or to height or to swerve or spin. But no one can bowl *simply* with speed, or simply with good direction or simply with height or swerve or spin: *some* importance, however slight, must, in practice, be attached to each of these factors, for all that the supporters of one team will speak of its "sheer-speed attack" (apparently neglecting other factors), while supporters of other teams coin phrases to emphasize other factors in bowling upon which their favored team concentrates its efforts.

To cover condition (4)—that the achievement our concept accredits is persistently vague—let us consider the particular case of the team which concentrates its efforts, and reposes its hopes for the championship, on a "sheer-speed attack." The task facing them is: can they put up an outstanding performance in this method and style of bowling, a performance which will make all other methods and styles look "not really bowling at all"? To succeed in this the bowlers in our team must evidently pay attention to circumstances, and modify their method of play as circumstances suggest or dictate. (We may imagine that certain grounds—or alleys—and certain lights are much more obviously favorable to "sheer-speed attack" than others.) But whatever the circumstances, our team strives to be acclaimed as "the champions" in virtue of its characteristic ("sheer-speed") method and style of bowling. In ostensibly favorable circumstances such acclamation could be backed by the judgment: "They are the champions—they have shown us what speed bowling *really* is." In ostensibly unfavorable circumstances it could be backed by: "They are the champions—they have shown us what speed can do when everything seems against it." In general no one can predict, at any given time, what level or what special adaptation of its own particular style—what bold raising or sagacious lowering of its achievement-targets—may strengthen any particular team's claim to be the champions.

So much for the four most important necessary preconditions[2] of a concept's being of essentially contested character, and for the further condition (5) which defines what it is to be a concept of this kind. But at this point the following objections may be raised: "All your definition does is to suggest the kind of situation in which people could claim to be using a concept of the kind you call 'essentially contested.' But the kind of situation you have described is indistinguishable from those situations in which people engage in apparently endless contests as to the right application of some epithet or slogan, which in fact serves simply to confuse two *different* concepts about whose proper application no one need have contested at all. The important question is how are these all-too-familiar cases to be distinguished from the artificial example which you have presented? To all appearances your concept of 'the champions' not only denotes consistently different sets of individuals (teams) according

---

[2] Are all four conditions necessary? I suggest that proof of this could be found along the following lines. Given conditions (2) and (3) we have the sort of situation where a multi-dimensional description or classification of certain facts is possible. But in any such situation, specific evidential or methodological reasons apart, it would be absurd to prefer one style of possible description or classification to the others. But substitute achievements for facts, i.e., an appraisive concept or classification for a purely naturalistic one, and the absurdity disappears, since for the purpose of moral or aesthetic persuasion one style of description or classification may very definitely be preferable to another which is *logically* equipollent with it. Here is a strong reason for thinking that condition (1) is necessary. But even in a situation which conforms to conditions (1), (2) and (3) it is conceivable that experience should establish *one* style of description as, again for the purpose of moral or aesthetic persuasion, universally more acceptable than any other. This result could hardly be expected, however, if condition (4) be added, i.e., if the kind of achievement which our concept or classification accredits is, in my sense, an "open" one; for what this condition ensures is, in terms of my artificial example, that *tomorrow's* circumstances may bring out hitherto latent virtues in the play of *any* of the contestant teams. There remains the possibility that the addition of condition (4) renders condition (1) superfluous. This could be maintained if, and only if, instances could be produced of a concept which conforms to my conditions (2), (3) and (4) and which is yet wholly nonappraisive in character. My suspicion is, however, that no *purely* naturalistic concept will be found conforming to my conditions (2), (3) and (4).

as it is used by different parties (supporters); it also connotes different achievements (in the way of different methods, strategies and styles favored by the different teams) according as it is used by different groups of supporters. Is there, then, any real ground for maintaining that it has a *single* meaning, that *could* be contested?"

The easy answer to this objection is that no one would conceivably refer to one team among others as "the champions" unless he believed his team to be playing better than all the others *at the same game*. The context of any typical use of "the champions" shows that it has thus far an unequivocal meaning as between its different (contestant) users. But to this answer the critic may retort: "But exactly the same situation appears to obtain wherever men dispute over the right use of what proves eventually to be a thoroughly confused concept, or better a thoroughly confusing term which cloaked the possibly perfectly consistent use of two or more concepts which only needed to be discriminated. Your definition of what it is to be an essentially contested concept may in a sense cover the kind of facts which your artificial example is meant to illustrate, but among them may well be the fact of a persistent delusion, viz., the deluded belief that the different teams *are* all playing the same game."

It turns out, then, that this objection is a request, not for further refinement of our definition of an essentially contested concept, but for an indication of the conditions in which the continued use of any such concept, as above defined, can be defended. And this is a perfectly fair request, since it is always reasonable to urge the parties contesting the rightful use of such a concept to bethink themselves with all seriousness, whether they are really alleging the same achievement. For instance, in our artificial example, might it not simply be said that T_1 is trying to put on a first class performance of (primarily) fast bowling; T_2 of (primarily) straight bowling, and so on, and that these quite proper but quite different aims of our different teams are not essentially, but only accidentally and as a result of persistent confusion, mutually contesting and contested?

I shall at once sketch the outlines of the required defence in terms of my artificial example, but must add that until it is interpreted in the live examples which follow, it may well seem somewhat specious. In defence, then, of the continued use of the concepts "championship" and "the champions" in my example I urge: each ot my teams could properly be said to be contesting for the *same* championship if, in every case, its peculiar method and style of playing had been derived by a process of imitation and adaptation from an *exemplar,* which might have the form either of one proto-type team of players, or of a succession (or tradition) of teams. This exemplar's way of playing must be recognized by all the contesting teams (and their supporters) to be "the way the game is to be played"; yet, because of the internally complex and variously de-scribable character of the exemplar's play, it is natural that different features in it should be differently weighted by different appraisers, and hence that our different teams should have come to hold their very different conceptions of how the game should be played. To this we should add that recognition or acceptance of the exemplar's achievement must have that "open" character which we have ascribed to every essentially contested concept. A certain kind of worthwhile achievement was presented, and our teams have all been seeking to revive or reproduce it in their play. But there can be no question of any purely mechanical repetition or reproduction of it. To follow an exemplar is to exert oneself to revive its (or his) way of doing things, not only to the utmost of one's ability, but to the utmost that circumstances, favorable or unfavorable, will allow.

Let us now illustrate this situation in terms of Team T_1 (with its "sheer-speed" attack) and its supporters. All members and supporters of this team are at one with all members and supporters of all other teams in acknowledging the authority of the exemplar; but in ap-praising the exemplar's achievement members and supporters of T_1 have concentrated their attention, primarily and predominantly, on the one factor of speed. They have conscientiously sustained and perhaps even advanced the exemplar's way of playing as circum-stances permitted in terms of their own appraisal of it. Members and supporters of T_1 are therefore assured that T_1 has played the game as it should be played. But just the same holds true, of course, of all the other contestant teams, together with their supporters.

At this point it is worth recalling that in our artificial example championship is not awarded on any quantitative system; we can now see how difficult, if not impossible, such a system would be to work, given the other conditions which we have laid down. For who is to say whether T_1's sustaining and advancing of the exemplar's way of playing is a better ("truer" or "more orthodox") achievement than that of, say, T_2, whose members have no doubt contended with quite different difficulties and exploited quite different advantages in their concentration upon the different factor of direction? In general, it would seem to be quite impossible to fix a *general prin-ciple* for deciding which of two such teams has really "done best"

—done best in its own peculiar way to advance or sustain the characteristic excellence revealed in the exemplar's play.

We have thus taken two steps in defence of the continued use of our essentially contested concept "the champions": (1) We have seen that each of our teams claims—and can point to facts which appear to support its claim—that its style of play embodies "the true line of descent" or "the right method of development" of the exemplar's play. (2) We have seen that there can be no general method or principle for deciding between the claims made by the different teams. To be sure, these steps do not amount to a justification of the claim of any particular team, viz., that *its* way of playing is the best. Indeed, if they did so the concept of "the champions" would cease to be an essentially contested one. Nevertheless, recalling the internally complex, and variously describable, and peculiarly "open" character of the exemplar's achievement, we must admit the following possibility: that this achievement could not have been revived and sustained or developed to the *optimum* which actual circumstances have allowed, except by the kind of continuous competition for acknowledged championship (and for acceptance of one particular criterion of "championship") which my artificial example was designed to illustrate. Thus Team T_1 could hardly have developed its sheer-speed attack to its present excellence had it not been aspiring to convert supporters from Team T_2, which in its turn could hardly have developed its skill in respect of direction had it not been aspiring to convert supporters . . . and so on for all the contestant teams. This result of continuous competition does not justify the claims of any one of our teams; but it might be said to justify, other things being equal, the combined employment of the essentially contested concept "the champions" by *all* the contesting teams.

Two comments on this line of defence may be added. (a) It has an obvious affinity to the now well-known theory of "competition" between rival scientific hypotheses, a theory which certainly does much to explain the apparently inherent progressiveness of the natural sciences. But its differences from this theory are as important as its affinity to it. Competition between scientific hypotheses works successfully largely because there are acknowledged general methods or principles for deciding between rival hypotheses, for all that these methods or principles may never be completely formalized or finally agreed. But nothing remotely like this is true in the case of essentially contested concepts; none of these, in the nature of the case, ever succumbs—as most scientific theories eventually do—to a definite or judicial knock-out. (b) The above defence of the continued use of an essentially contested concept is conditional in the extreme. It is introduced as a possibility, which the facts in certain cases may at once preclude. For example it might turn out that continued use of two or more rival versions of an essentially contested concept would have the effect of utterly frustrating the kind of activity and achievement which it was the job of this concept (in and through all the rival contestant versions) to appraise—and through positive appraisal to help to sustain. Even in more favorable cases, the question whether in fact competition between rival claimants has sustained or developed the original exemplar's achievement to the optimum, will usually be a very difficult one to decide. This is the first import of the phrase "other things being equal" in this connection. But again, even where the question could be answered affirmatively with regard to the kind of achievement in question, the cost of sustaining and developing it competitively may well be judged too high in the light of its more general effects. In this connection, our artificial example from the happy field or sport was an unusually favorable one. It suggested one main and at least harmless result —the sustaining and developing of a number of competitively connected athletic skills. But suppose the pursuit of championship in our example were to result in the impoverishment of all the layers and supporters (through neglect of their proper business), or in the formation of savage political cleavages between different teams and their supporters—then our reaction to it would be very different. In general, the above defence of the continued use of any essentially contested concept is evidently subject to very stringent conditions.

To sum up this part of our discussion. Conditions (1) to (5) as stated on page 125 above give us the formally defining conditions of essential contestedness. But they fail to distinguish the essentially contested concept from the kind of concept which can be shown, as a result of analysis or experiment, to be radically confused. In order to make this distinction, which is in effect to justify the continued use of any essentially contested concept, it is necessary to add two further conditions. These are (6) the derivation of any such concept from an original exemplar whose authority is acknowledged by all the contestant users of the concept, and (7) the probability or plausibility, in appropriate senses of these terms, of the claim that the continuous competition for acknowledgement as between the contestant users of the concept, enables the original exemplar's achievement to be sustained and/or developed in optimum fashion.

Some Live Examples

The examples I choose are the concepts of Art, of Democracy, of Social Justice, and that of the adherence to, or participation in, a particular religion. None of these concepts conforms with perfect precision to the seven conditions I have set out above. But do they conform to my conditions sufficiently closely for us to agree that their essential contestedness explains—or goes a very long way towards explaining—the ways they function in characteristic aesthetic, political and religious arguments? This is the test question which I believe my account of them will satisfy.

Of the concepts just mentioned the fourth seems to me to satisfy most nearly perfectly my several conditions. Consider, as illustration of it, the phrase "a Christian life." Clearly this is an appraisive term; on reflection it can be seen, equally clearly, to signify an achievement that is internally complex, variously describable and "open" in the senses which I have given to those terms. Too often, if not always, it is used both "aggressively" and "defensively." That any proper use of it conforms to the first of my two justifying conditions, (6) above, is obvious; whilst that it conforms to my condition (7) might be agreed (though no doubt with many different qualifying conditions) not only by liberal Christians, but by liberal spirits of other (or even of no) religious persuasions.

The most questionable case is that of its conformity to condition (5). Is the phrase "a Christian life" necessarily used both aggressively and defensively? The familiar pattern of the history of Christianity is certainly that of one dominant church, in any area or in any epoch, *and* usually a number of dissenting or protesting sects. But is there anything inherently necessary in this pattern? Is the Christian kingdom, here below also, essentially one of many mansions? Conformity to my conditions (1) to (4) and to my condition (6) cannot be said, in this or in any instance, to *entail* such a conclusion. But it makes it extremely *likely* that such a conclusion will be found to hold; and given its historical development to date—which is something that Christianity (in this like any other great religion) can never possibly shed—its contested character, or the aggressive and defensive use of many of its key doctrines and principles, would appear to belong inherently to it *now*.

Having said this I do not propose to press this example any further, partly because of my ignorance of the relevant apologetic literature, but chiefly because the most important question it raises is one which I shall try to deal with later in a more general form. This is the question, which would be raised by any positivistically minded critic of any religion, whether the so-called arguments by which adherents of one creed seek to convert adherents of other creeds are in any proper sense arguments at all.

Let us next consider the concept of Art. As with our previous example so here, clarification requires that we view this concept with the historian's as much as with the logician's eye; for perhaps the most interesting fact about it is the brevity of its history, the comparatively recent date of its "arrival" as a theoretical concept. Nevertheless, during that history it has succeeded in being continuously contested, and for reasons that are not hard to find. Running again through our five necessary conditions of essential contestedness we can easily agree: (1) Art as we use the term today is mainly, if not exclusively, an appraisive term. (2) The kind of achievement it accredits is always internally complex. (3) This achievement has proved to be variously describable—largely, if not solely, because at different times and in different circles it has seemed both natural and justifiable to describe the phenomena of Art with a dominant emphasis now on the work of Art (Art-product) itself, now on the response of the audience or spectator, now on the aim and inspiration of the artist, now on the tradition within which the artist works, now on the general fact of communication between the artist, via art-product, and audience. (4) Artistic achievement, or the persistence of artistic activity is always "open" in character in the sense that, at any one stage in its history, no one can predict or prescribe what new development of current art-forms may come to be regarded as of properly artistic worth. (5) Intelligent artists and critics will readily agree that the term Art and its derivatives are used, for the most part, both aggressively and defensively.

I must admit that my first justifying condition—derivation from a single generally acknowledged exemplar (in this case a single tradition of art) cannot be simply or directly applied. Clearly there have been different, and very often quite independent, artistic traditions. Nevertheless, I think that in any intelligent discussion of works of art or of artistic valuation, it is fairly easy to see what particular artistic tradition or set of traditions is being regarded as the "exemplar term." Finally it could at least be argued that the stimulating effects of competition between different aesthetic viewpoints, or different styles of description of aesthetic values, have provided a sufficient justification of the continued use of Art as an essentially contested term.

I think it is worth adding, to meet the objections of those who would decry the term Art as a useless blanket-term, that a supporting account could be given of the actual use in criticism of a number of relatively specific aesthetic terms. I will mention only one example: the notion of coloration. From different aesthetic viewpoints coloration, considered as an apprasive term, may be used to refer predominantly either to the arrangement of pigments on a surface, or to the use of pigments to convey certain *other* spatial effects, e.g., massiveness, distance, etc., or to their use to represent or suggest certain forms found in nature, or to express something peculiar (individual, novel, important) in the artist's general way of seeing things. This being so, it is not difficult to see that the notion of coloration is in fact used in an essentially contested manner, even if this fact is not admitted by the majority of critics and aestheticians.

Coming now to the concept of Democracy, I want first to make clear what uses of it, in political discussion, are *not* here to be discussed. Sometimes in a political argument actual political conditions or actions are referred to and then the question is put: "Can you call *that* democratic?" or "Is *this* an example for your democracy?" But questions of actual practice, vindicating or belying certain particular uses of the term "democracy" are not here our concern. Again, when commending certain political arrangements or in criticizing others, political spokesmen sometimes make use of *theoretical* considerations (drawn perhaps from political science, perhaps from political philosophy), which appear to show that from the arrangements in question democratic results can be expected to follow, or alternatively are most unlikely to, or even could not conceivably follow. But such theory-inspired uses or mentions of the term democracy are not here our concern. Both the above uses presuppose a more elementary use in which it can be said to express (and usually today to express approval of) certain political aspirations which have been embodied in countless slave, peasant, national and middle-class revolts and revolutions, as well as in scores of national constitutions and party records and programs. These aspirations are evidently centered in a demand for increased equality: or, to put it negatively, they are advanced against governments and social orders whose aim is to prolong gross forms of *in*equality. To be sure, when thus conceived, the concept of democracy is extremely vague, but not, I think, hopelessly so, as is, for instance, the concept of the "cause of right." Its vagueness reflects its actual inchoate condition of growth; and if we want to understand its condition, and control its practical and logical vagaries, the first step, I believe, is to recognize its essentially contested character. Let us therefore once again run through my list of defining and justifying conditions.

(1) The concept of democracy which we are discussing is appraisive; indeed many would urge that during the last one hundred and fifty years it has steadily established itself as *the* appraisive political concept *par excellence*. Questions of efficiency and security apart, the primary question on any major policy decision has come to be: Is it democratic? By contrast, the concept of liberty, or more accurately, of particular liberties deserving protection irrespective of their democratic spread or appeal, appears steadily to have lost ground.

(2) and (3) The concept of democracy which we are discussing is internally complex in such a way that any democratic achievement (or program) admits of a variety of descriptions in which its different aspects are graded in different orders of importance. I list as examples of different aspects (a) Democracy means primarily the power of the majority of citizens to choose (and remove) governments—a power which would seem to involve, anyhow in larger communities, something like the institution of parties competing for political leadership; (b) Democracy means primarily equality of all citizens, irrespective of race, creed, sex, etc., to attain to positions of political leadership and responsibility; (c) Democracy means primarily the continuous active participation of citizens in political life at all levels, i.e., it is real when, and in so far as, there really is *self*-government.

Of these descriptions (b) and (c) emphasize features of democracy which clearly can exist in greater or less degree and are therefore liable to be differently placed for relative importance. But does not description (a) state an absolute requirement and therefore a necessary condition of paramount importance—perhaps even a sufficient condition—of a democratic society? We of the western tradition commonly claim this; but I believe our claim to be confused, for all that our democratic practice may have been, to date, none the worse for that.[3]

---

[3] I say confused, because it seems to me that the claim that description (a) is of absolute, paramount (and perhaps also of logically sufficient) character, is commonly grounded upon two *liberal* principles or beliefs, viz., (1) that those political liberties that are enjoyed by all (or almost all) our citizens deserve protection primarily because *all* traditionally accepted liberties (no matter how restricted the enjoyment of them) are things that *prima facie* deserve protection, and (2) that the existence of a wide variety of liberties (enjoyed by different ranges of our citizens) has been historically and remains today a *necessary* condition of our specifically *democratic* values and achievements. Both these claims, I would

Suppose a society which answers in high degree to the conditions required by descriptions (b) and (c). In such a society government might reasonably be expected to show itself responsive, in considerable degree, to movements of popular opinion. Yet this result does not necessarily require constitutionally recognized means (e.g., universal and secret ballot and the existence of competitive parties) for the wholesale removal of governments. The practice of certain churches which claim to satisfy proper democratic demands, here shows a curious analogy to those governments which insist on their democratic character while denying their citizens the right of "free election" on the western pattern. For this reason, as well as for others which space forbids me to elaborate here, I conclude that the popular conception of democracy conforms to my conditions (2) and (3) for essential contestedness.

(4) The concept of democracy which we are discussing is "open" in character. Politics being the art of the possible, democratic targets will be raised or lowered as circumstances alter, and democratic achievements are always judged in the light of such alterations. (5) The concept of democracy which we are discussing is used both aggressively and defensively. This hardly requires discussion—except by those who repudiate the suggestion that there is any single general use of the term "democracy." My reply here is that such people neglect the possibility of a single general use made up, essentially, of a number of mutually contesting and contested uses of it. (6) These uses claim the authority of an exemplar, i.e., of a long tradition (perhaps a number of historically independent but sufficiently similar traditions) of demands, aspirations, revolts and reforms of a common *anti-in*egalitarian character; and to see that the vagueness of this tradition in no way affects its influence as an exemplar, we need only recall how many and various political movements claim to have drawn their inspiration from the French Revolution. (7) Can we add, finally, that continuous competition for acknowledgement between rival uses of the popular concept of

---

say, reflect our grasp of a particular historical truth of immense importance, viz., as to how democracy has taken root and flourished in the west. But if they are put forward as universal political truths expressing the necessary conditions of *any* genuinely democratic aspirations or achievements, then they are surely open to question. To many people in the world today they must seem indeed, not so much questionable as utterly—and in a sense insultingly—irrelevant to their actual situation. What is the relevance of a Burkian philosophy of political liberties to the great majority of Asians and Africans today?

democracy seems likely to lead to an *optimum* development of the vague aims and confused achievements of the democratic tradition? Is it not, rather, more likely to help fan the flames of conflict, already sufficiently fed by other causes, between those groups of men and nations that contest its proper use? It is not the job of the present analysis, or of political philosophy in general, to offer particular predictions or advice on this kind of issue. But our present analysis does prompt the question, for which parallels could be provided by my other live examples, and which I shall try to answer in generalized form below, viz., In what way should we expect current dog fights over the concept of democracy to be affected if its essentially contested character were recognized by all concerned?

Whereas the concepts of religion, of art and of democracy would seem to admit, under my condition (3), of an indefinite number of possible descriptions, the concept of social justice as popularly used today seems to admit of only two.[4] Of these the first rests on the ideas of merit and commutation: justice consists in the institution and application of those social arrangements whereby the meritorious individual receives his commutative due. The second rests upon, in the sense of presupposing, the ideas (or ideals) of cooperation, to provide the necessities of a worthwhile human life, and of distribution of products to assure such a life to all who cooperate. It is natural to take these two descriptions as characteristic of two facets of contemporary morality, which might be labelled liberal and socialist respectively. But in fact these two facets would seem to appear in any morality or moral teaching worthy of the name: witness, e.g., the opposed lessons of the parable of the talents and the parable of the vineyard, or, on a humbler plane, contrast the encouragement one gives to children now to show their worth, now to pitch in for the sake of the family or group or side.

It is the sheer duality of these opposed uses that is of particular interest, since it suggests a bridge between those appraisive concepts which are variously describable and essentially contested and those whose everyday use appears to be uniquely describable and universally acknowledged. Such are the central concepts of ethics; and the bearing upon these of my suggested new grouping of concepts is the third question which I reserve for separate discussion below.

[4] *Cf.* my "Liberal Morality and Social Morality" in *Philosophy*, XXIV, No. 91 (1950), 318-334.

Outstanding Questions

I shall now assume that each of my live examples conforms sufficiently closely to my conditions (1)-(7) for it to be agreed that my proposed new grouping of concepts goes some way towards explaining them. But what further results can we expect from it? To answer this I turn to the three questions which I left outstanding in the previous section, on the ground that they would usefully admit of a more generalized treatment.

(1) **Are** the endless disputes to which the use of any essentially contested concept give rise *genuine* disputes, i.e., of such a character that the notions of evidence, cogency and rational persuasion can properly be applied to them? This is, in effect, the question whether there is such a thing as "the logic" of *conversion* either in the religious or aesthetic or in the political and moral fields. Are *some* conversions in any of these fields of such a kind that they can be described as logically justified or defensible? Or on the contrary, are conversions in these fields always changes of viewpoint which can indeed be effected or engineered by appropriate methods, and can be causally explained by adducing relevant facts and generalizations, but only in such ways that the idea of logical "justification" is inappropriate to them? Our previous discussion has sufficiently emphasized one all-important point: viz., that if the notion of logical justification can be applied only to such theses and arguments as can be presumed capable of gaining in the long run universal agreement, the disputes to which the uses of any essentially contested concept give rise are not genuine or rational disputes at all. Our first question, then, is to decide whether conformity to this condition —the possibility of obtaining universal agreement—provides a necessary criterion of the genuineness of arguments or disputes of all kinds. Now an affirmative answer to this question certainly requires some special defence; for the notion of possible ultimate universal agreement is a highly sophisticated one and does not figure among the familiarly recognized criteria of rational justification. Moreover, I would claim that those who have urged us to accept an affirmative answer here have entirely neglected the existence of essentially contested concepts, and have failed to examine in any detail the peculiar structures of the arguments to which their uses give rise. Pending such examination, therefore, I conclude that this first possible form of the objection need not cause us any great worry.

But now the objection can be put on more general grounds, viz., that, as we have explicitly confessed, it is quite impossible to find a *general principle* for deciding which of two contestant uses of an essentially contested concept really "uses it best." If no such principle can be found or fixed, then how can the arguments of the contestants in such a dispute be subject to logical appraisal? My answer is that even where a general principle may be unobtainable for deciding, in a manner that would or might conceivably win ultimate agreement, which of a number of contestant uses of a given concept is its "best use," it may yet be possible to explain or show the rationality of a *given individual's* continued use (or in the more dramatic case of conversion his *change of use*) of the concept in question.

To show how this is possible let me revert, yet once again, to my artificial example and consider the supporters of three contestant teams T_1, T_2, and T_3. And for simplicity let us assume that the style of play of T_2 can be said to stand midway between the styles of T_1 and T_3. Let us recall, too, that in each of these groups of supporters there will always be wavering or marginal individuals, who are more than usually aware of the appeals—the characteristic excellences—of teams other than that which at the moment they favor and support. Let us concentrate on an individual I_2, at present a marginal supporter of T_2. A particular performance of Team T_1, or some shrewd appraisive comment from one of T_1's supporters suddenly makes him realize much more completely than heretofore the justice of T_1's claim to be sustaining and advancing the original exemplar team's style of play in "the best possible way." This tips the scale for him and he is converted to being a supporter of T_1. But now we may assume that the same particular performance (or shrewd appraisive comment) has had a comparable—though not so dramatically effective—influence upon other staunch supporters of T_2. It has slightly shaken them, we might say. At least it has made them aware that, in comparable circumstances T_2 must make a comparably effective adaptation of *its* style of play if it is to keep their unwavering support. Further, we may assume that although supporters of T_3 are less shaken by the particular performance, they have at least been made to "sit up and take notice"; and similarly, with decreasing degrees of force for supporters of other teams whose styles of play are still remoter from that of T_1.

Put less artificially, what I am claiming is that a certain piece of evidence or argument put forward by one side in an apparently endless dispute can be recognized to have a definite logical force, even by those whom it entirely fails to win over or convert to the side in question; and that when this is the case, the conversion of a hitherto wavering opponent of the side in question can be seen to be *justifiable*—not simply expectable in the light of known relevant psychological or sociological laws—given the waverer's previous state of information and given the grounds on which he previously supported one side and opposed the other. It is for this reason that we can distinguish more or less intellectually respectable conversions from those of a more purely emotional, or yet those of a wholly sinister kind. To be sure, our previous wavering opponent of one use of an essentially contested concept would not be justified in transferring his allegiance in the circumstances outlined if he were able, for an indefinite length of time, to withhold his support *from any of its possible uses,* i.e., to take up an entirely uncommitted attitude. But as in our artificial example, so in life this possibility is often precluded. The exigencies of living commonly demand that "he who is not for us is against us," or that he who hesitates to throw in his support or make his contribution on one side or the other is lost—not just to one of the sides that might have claimed his support—but to the game and to the day. From this point of view "the logic of conversion" from one contested use of an essentially contested concept to another is on all fours with the logic of every unique decision: and as in the latter more general case, so in that which concerns us here, there can be little question but that greater or lesser degrees of rationality can be properly and naturally attributed to one continued use, or one change of use, than to others.

Two points may be added to reinforce this account. It has usually been asserted by "attitude-moralists" that the sole significant content of any moral dispute must concern the facts, the empirically testable facts, of the matter in question. It is important to contrast this assertion with our account of the conversion of the individual I_2. What I_2 recognizes in my account, is a fact if you like, but not a mere empirical observandum. It is, rather, the fact that a particular achievement (of T_1) revives and realizes, as it were in fuller relief, some already recognized feature of an already valued style of performance, i.e., that of the original exemplar. Because of this particular performance I_2 sees, or claims to see, more clearly and fully *why* he has acknowledged and followed the exemplar's style of performance all along. The scales are tipped for him not, or at least not only, by some psychologically explainable kink of his temperament, not by some observandum whose sheer occurrence all observers must acknowledge, but by his recognition of a value which, given his particular marginal appraisive situation, is conclusive for him, although it is merely impressive or surprising or worth noticing for others.

While insisting that there may be this much objectivity in the grounds of any particular conversion, we may nevertheless agree with "attitude-moralists" that fundamental differences of attitude, of a kind for which no logical justification can be given, must also lie back of the kind of situation which we have just discussed. Why should one style of play (as in our artificial example) appeal to one group of supporters and another style to a second group? Why should one facet of Democracy or of the Christian Message appeal so strongly to one type or group or communion, another to a second? At any given stage in the history of the continued uses of any essentially contested concept, it will no doubt be necessary to call upon psychological or sociological history or the known historical facts of a person's or group's background, to explain their present preferences and adherences. But to admit this is not to deny the existence, or at least the possibility, of logically appraisable factors in an individual's use, or change of use, of a particular contested concept.

Our second outstanding question may be stated as follows: In what ways should we expect recognition of the essentially contested character of a given concept to affect its future uses by different contestant parties?

Two preliminary points must be made: (1) It is important to distinguish clearly such recognition—a somewhat sophisticated "higher order" intellectual feat—from the everyday "lower order" recognition that one is using a given concept both aggressively and defensively. The difference is between recognizing that one has, and presumably will continue to have, opponents, and recognizing that this is an essential feature of the activity one is pursuing. The obvious advantage of the "higher order" recognition is (assuming my present analysis to be acceptable) that it makes the parties concerned aware of an important truth. But this will be a truth of high order, whose significance can best be understood in terms of its important everyday applications. The answer we are seeking must enable us to meet the following questions: How will a Christian of denomination X be likely to be affected in respect of his intellectual allegiance to X (and consequently repudiation of Y and Z) by the recognition which we are here discussing? Similarly, how will the student of the arts be affected by recognizing that different groups of critics not only disagree, but in the nature of the case must be expected to disagree in their fundamental viewpoints? And so on for the other cases. (2) It is also important to stress that the results with which we are here concerned are not to be of a predictable or causally explainable character. The practical and theoretical operations which recognition of a concept as essentially contested makes possible are logically appraisable and justifiable operations, such as we would expect from a reasonable being, for all that, for special psychological or social causes, a given individual may fail to entertain them. It is therefore neither redundant nor irrelevant to insist that examination of these results is an important part of our analysis.

Part of the answer to our question seems to be this. Recognition of a given concept as essentially contested implies recognition of rival uses of it (such as oneself repudiates) as not only logically possible and humanly "likely," but as of permanent potential critical value to one's own use or interpretation of the concept in question; whereas to regard any rival use as anathema, perverse, bestial or lunatic means, in many cases, to submit oneself to the chronic human peril of underestimating the value of one's opponents' positions. One very desirable consequence of the required recognition in any proper instance of essential contestedness might therefore be expected to be a marked raising of the level of quality of arguments in the disputes of the contestant parties. And this would mean *prima facie,* a justification of the continued competition for support and acknowledgement between the various contesting parties.

But as against this optimistic view the following darker considerations might be urged. So long as contestant users of any essentially contested concept believe, however deludedly, that their own use of it is the only one that can command honest and informed approval, they are likely to persist in the hope that they will ultimately persuade and convert all their opponents by logical means. But once let the truth out of the bag—i.e., the essential contestedness of the concept in question—then this harmless if deluded hope may well be replaced by a ruthless decision to cut the cackle, to damn the heretics and to exterminate the unwanted.

This consideration might give us pause until we recall that spokesmen of Reason have always brought peril as well as light to their hearers. The consequences of the present requirement—recognition of essential contestedness in appropriate cases—is in this respect nothing extraordinary. In any case tne above objection gives too much credit to the "reasonableness" of those who will employ reason only given the prospect of eventual knockout victory. The relevant fact is, rather, that evil men always want quick victories;

they prefer the elimination of opponents today to their conversion
—or even their adequate indoctrination—tomorrow. Furthermore,
what is being brought to our notice by the present objection is
simply a possible *causal* consequence, such as is in no way logically
justifiable, of recognition of a given concept as essentially contested, and has therefore no logical relevance to our present analysis.

My last outstanding question may be put as follows: What are
the bearings of my suggested new grouping of concepts upon the
central normative and appraisive concepts of ethics? Or, more
specifically: if certain very important appraisive concepts (e.g., those
of democracy and social justice) turn out to be of an essentially
contested character, how should this affect the common assumption
that the central concepts of ethics are uniquely describable and
such as to command universal assent?

Clearly I cannot attempt even to state, still less to defend, a convincing answer to these questions, in the space left at my disposal.
They are, nevertheless, probably the most important questions that
the present paper raises: and I shall therefore attempt a brief further
restatement of them, to show their bearing upon the terms "moral
goodness" and "duty." Then I shall leave my readers to draw their
own conclusions and (should they be interested) to guess at mine.

(a) Moralists commonly claim that, among the many overlapping
senses of the word "good," we can all detect *one* use of it, its fundamental use in moral discussion, about whose propriety in any particular situation no two rational (or morally developed) persons
will disagree, given that they share precisely the same factual
knowledge of the situation in question. Certain saintly characters, or
supremely noble actions, e.g., self-sacrifice, are usually cited as illustrations. But these, like other supreme sources of illumination, are
apt, through their unquestionable force, only to intensify the surrounding darkness. *Some* of our moral appraisals command universal assent, but by no means all do so. It is of the first importance
to insist that we also use the word "good" (or its near-equivalents
and derivatives) with a definitely moral, but just as definitely questionable force: witness such phrases as "a good Christian," "a good
patriot," "a good democrat," "a good painter" (when we mean a sin-
cere, sensitive, intelligent, always rewarding—but not necessarily a
"great" or a "fine" painter), "a good husband," and so on. In all
these uses, it seems perfectly clear, our concept of the activity in and
through which the man's goodness is said to be manifested, is of an
essentially contested character. "He was a good Christian" says X,
to which Y replies tartly "I suppose you mean he was a good Church-

man." "He was a good husband" says X, and Y replies "Agreed that
he was faithful, sober, hard-working and never raised his hand or
his voice, BUT. . . ." Now I have yet to read a philosophical
moralist who took seriously the difficulty which these examples
illustrate.

(b) To do one's duty in a particular situation involves, we would
all agree, some reference to what any other rational being would do
"in a similar situation." But many of our duties arise out of our
adherence to one particular use of an essentially contested concept,
e.g., social justice. Now the question arises: Shall reference to such
adherence be counted as a necessary part of any "similar situation"?
If so, then the universality criterion of duty is rendered trivial: if
not, then, anyhow in a great many very important issues, it becomes
inapplicable. But can either of these results satisfy any perceptive
and serious moralist?

Concluding Remarks

I should like in conclusion to anticipate two lines of criticism:
(1) It may be complained that despite all its references to "reasonableness," to the "logic of conversion," etc., this paper is only a dis-
guised betrayal of reason, a further contribution to what Mr.
Hampshire has so aptly called "the new obscurantism." To find reasonableness in the pursuit of inevitably endless conflicts—is not this
as paradoxical and as dangerous as to find it in the dictates of the
heart and the blood or in the actual march of history? Reason,
according to so many great philosophical voices, is essentially something which demands and deserves universal assent—the manifestation of whatever makes for unity among men and/or the constant
quest for such beliefs as could theoretically be accepted as satis-
factory by all men. This account of reason may be adequate so long
as our chief concern is with the use or manifestation of reason in
science; but it fails completely as a description of those elements of
reason that make possible *discussions* of religious, political and artistic problems. Since the Enlightenment a number of brilliant
thinkers seem positively to have exulted in emphasizing the *ir*-
rational elements in our thinking in these latter fields. My purpose
in this paper has been to combat, and in some measure correct, this
dangerous tendency. (2) It might be objected that my proposed
new grouping of concepts simply presents in fake logical guise
certain facts *about* our uses of a number of concepts—facts which
might prove important to historians of ideas and sociologists, but

which in no way explain to us what those uses *are*. In general (the supposed objector would continue) there are two quite distinct senses in which we can be said to understand a concept or theory or other tool of thought: first, the "logical" sense, in which to understand it means (a) to conform to, and (b) to be able to state, the rules governing its proper use; and second, the "historical" sense, in which to understand it means to know (something about) the whole gamut of conditions that have led to, and that now sustain, the way we use it. Now to confuse these two senses is to prolong, in a rather sophisticated form, the "historicist fallacy." I agree, of course, that we must avoid confusing these two senses; but it seems to me equally important that we should see aright the connection between them in different sorts of case.

This connection is most tenuous, when the appropriate use of a concept would appear to mean simply, its use for deductive purposes: as, for example, when the meaning of any well-established concept of the physical sciences is equated with its predictive power. In this kind of case, clarification or improved understanding of a concept would naturally be taken to mean improvement in one's skill and confidence in using it—thanks to, e.g., a full and clear statement of the rules governing its use. But quite clearly this account will not serve for all concepts, and in particular not for appraisive concepts. Admittedly, the use of some appraisive concepts may appear to be predictive; but this appearance is, I think, always deceptive, and is due to the fact that the *subject* of the appraisal (a man, a character, a practice, a *kind* of action) is such that any reference to it is always latently predictive. Thus, to call a man wise is in a sense to predict his behavior; but it is not specifically in virtue of *what is predicted or predictable* about him that we term him "wise," nor yet because his known behavior can be projected into the future, or for that matter into the unknown past. Similarly, we call X a good poet because he has written some good poems—but this involves no prediction that he will produce more, and no retrodiction to hidden (or burnt) adolescent masterpieces. Quite simply, to appraise something positively is to assert that it fulfills certain generally recognized standards: and this being so, we should expect clarification or improved understanding of an appraisive concept to be obtained in a very different way from clarification of any concept of science.

But how then can it be obtained? I shall simply assert my view that such clarification—if it is to be worthy of the name—must *include,* not simply consideration of different uses of a given appraisive concept *as we use it today,* but consideration of such instances as display its growth and development. For, if we want to see *just what* we are doing, when we apply a given appraisive concept, then one way of learning this is by asking from what vaguer or more confused or more restricted version (or ancestor) our currently accepted version of the concept in question has been derived. Commonly we come to see more precisely what a given scientific concept means by contrasting its deductive powers with those of other closely related concepts: in the case of an appraisive concept, we can best see more precisely what it means by comparing and contrasting our uses of it now with other earlier uses of it or its progenitors, i.e., by considering how it came to be. If this be historicism, I cannot see that it is fallacious; and if it be acceptable in connection with appraisive concepts, then it is well worth asking where the limit of its acceptability should be drawn.

The Theory of Meaning

by GILBERT RYLE

We can all use the notion of *meaning*. From the moment we begin to learn to translate English into French and French into English, we realize that one expression does or does not mean the same as another. But we use the notion of meaning even earlier than that. When we read or hear something in our own language which we do not understand, we wonder what it means and ask to have its meaning explained to us. The ideas of understanding, misunderstanding and failing to understand what is said already contain the notion of expressions having and lacking specifiable meanings.

It is, however, one thing to ask, as a child might ask, What, if anything, is meant by "vitamin," or "abracadabra" or "(a + b)² = a² + b² + 2ab"? It is quite another sort of thing to ask What are meanings? It is, in the same way, one thing to ask, as a child might ask, What can I buy for this shilling? and quite another sort of thing to ask What is purchasing-power? or What are exchange-values?

Now answers to this highly abstract question, What are meanings? have, in recent decades, bulked large in philosophical and logical discussions. Preoccupation with the theory of meaning could be described as the occupational disease of twentieth-century Anglo-Saxon and Austrian philosophy. We need not worry whether or not it is a disease. But it might be useful to survey the motives and the major results of this preoccupation.

Incidentally it is worth noticing that many of these issues were explicitly canvassed—and some of them conclusively settled—in certain of Plato's later Dialogues, and in the logical and other works of Aristotle. Some of them, again, were dominant issues in the late Middle Ages and later still with Hobbes; and some of them, thickly or thinly veiled in the psychological terminology of "ideas," stirred uneasily inside British epistemology between Locke and John Stuart Mill. But I shall not, save for one or two back-references, discuss the early history of these issues.

The shopkeeper, the customer, the banker and the merchant are ordinarily under no intellectual pressure to answer or even ask the abstract questions What is purchasing-power? and What are exchange-values? They are interested in the prices of things, but not yet in the abstract question What is the real nature of that which is common to two articles of the same price? Similarly, the child who tries to follow a conversation on an unfamiliar topic, and the translator who tries to render Thucydides into English are interested in what certain expressions mean. But they are not necessarily interested in the abstract questions What is it for an expression to have a meaning? or What is the nature and status of that which an expression and its translation or paraphrase are both the vehicles? From what sort of interests, then, do we come to ask this sort of question? Doubtless there are many answers. I shall concentrate on two of them which I shall call "the Theory of Logic" and "the Theory of Philosophy." I shall spend a good long time on the first; not so long on the second.

The Theory of Logic

The logician, in studying the rules of inference has to talk of the components of arguments, namely their premisses and conclusions and to talk of them in perfectly general terms. Even when he adduces concrete premisses and conclusions, he does so only to illustrate the generalities which are his proper concern. In the same way, he has to discuss the types of separable components or the types of distinguishable features of these premise types and conclusion types, since it is sometimes on such components or features of premises and conclusions that the inferences from and to them pivot.

Now the same argument may be expressed in English or in French or in any other language; and if it is expressed in English, there may still be hosts of different ways of wording it. What the logician is exploring is intended to be indifferent to these differences of wording. He is concerned with what is said by a premiss-sentence or a conclusion-sentence, not with how it is worded.

So, if not in the prosecution of his inquiry, at least in his explanations of what he is doing, he has to declare that his subject matter consists not of the sentences and their ingredient words in which arguments are expressed, but of the propositions or judgments and their constituent terms, ideas, or concepts of which the sentences and words are the vehicles. Sometimes he may say that his subject matter consists of sentence-meanings and their constituent word-meanings or phrase-meanings, though this idiom is interesingly re-pellent. Why it is repellent we shall, I hope, see later on. So in giving this sort of explanation of his business, he is talking *about* meanings, where in the prosecution of that business he is just operating *upon* them.

For our purposes it is near enough true to say that the first influential discussion of the notion of meaning given by a modern logician was that with which John Stuart Mill opens his *System of Logic* (1843). He acknowledges debts both to Hobbes and to the Schoolmen, but we need not trace these borrowings in detail.

Mill's contributions to Formal or Symbolic Logic were negligible. It was not he but his exact contemporaries, Boole and de Morgan, and his immediate successors, Jevons, Venn, Carroll, McColl and Peirce who, in the English-speaking world, paved the way for Rus-sell. On the other hand, it is difficult to exaggerate the influence which he exercised, for good and for ill, upon British and Con-tinental philosophers; and we must include among these philoso-phers the Symbolic Logicians as well, in so far as they have philoso-phized about their technical business. In particular, Mill's theory of meaning set the questions, and in large measure, determined their answers for thinkers as different as Brentano, in Austria; Meinong and Husserl, who were pupils of Brentano; Bradley, Jevons, Venn, Frege, James, Peirce, Moore and Russell. This ex-traordinary achievement was due chiefly to the fact that Mill was original in producing a doctrine of meaning at all. The doctrine that he produced was immediately influential, partly because a doc-trine was needed and partly because its inconsistencies were trans-parent. Nearly all of the thinkers whom I have listed were in vehement opposition to certain parts of Mill's doctrine, and it was the other parts of it from which they often drew their most effective weapons.

Mill, following Hobbes's lead, starts off his account of the notion of meaning by considering single words. As we have to learn the alphabet before we can begin to spell, so it seemed natural to suppose that the meanings of sentences are compounds of the com-ponents, which are the meanings of their ingredient words. Word-meanings are atoms, sentence-meanings are molecules. I say that it seemed natural, but I hope soon to satisfy you that it was a tragi-cally false start. Next Mill, again following Hobbes's lead, takes it for granted that all words, or nearly all words, are names, and this, at first, sounds very tempting. We know what it is for "Fido" to be the name of a particular dog, and for "London" to be the name of a particular town. There, in front of us, is the dog or the town which has the name, so here, one feels, there is no mystery. We have just the familiar relation between a thing and its name. The assimilation of all or most other single words to names gives us, accordingly, a cosy feeling. We fancy that we know where we are. The dog in front of us is what the word "Fido" stands for, the town we visited yesterday is what the word "London" stands for. So the classification of all or most single words as names makes us feel that what a word means is in all cases some manageable thing that that word is the name of. Meanings, at least word meanings, are nothing abstruse or remote, they are, *prima facie,* ordinary things and happenings like dogs and towns and battles.

Mill goes further. Sometimes the grammatical subject of a sentence is not a single word but a many-worded phrase, like "the present Prime Minister" or "the first man to stand on the summit of Mt. Everest." Mill has no qualms in classifying complex expressions like these also as names, what he calls "many-worded names." There do not exist proper names for everything we want to talk about; and sometimes we want to talk about something or somebody whose proper name, though it exists, is unknown to us. So descriptive phrases are coined by us to do duty for proper names. But they are still, according to Mill, names, though the tempting and in fact prevailing interpretation of this assertion differs importantly from what Mill usually wanted to convey. For, when Mill calls a word or phrase a "name," he is using "name" not, or not always, quite in the ordinary way. Sometimes he says that for an expression to be a name it must be able to be used as the subject or the predicate of a subject-predicate sentence—which lets in, e.g. adjectives as names. Sometimes his requirements are more stringent. A name is an expression which can be the subject of a subject-predicate sentence—which leaves only nouns, pronouns and substantival phrases. "Name," for him, does not mean merely "proper name." He often resisted temptations to which he subjected his successors.

Before going any further, I want to make you at least suspect that this initially congenial equation of words and descriptive phrases with names is from the outset a monstrous howler—if, like some of Mill's successors, though unlike Mill himself, we do systematically construe "name" on the model of "proper name." The assumption of the truth of this equation has been responsible for a large number of radical absurdities in philosophy in general and the philosophy of logic in particular. It was a fetter round the ankles of Meinong, from which he never freed himself. It was a fetter round the ankles of Frege, Moore and Russell, who all, sooner or later, saw that without some big emendations, the assumption led inevitably to fatal impasses. It was, as he himself says in his new book, a fetter round the ankles of Wittgenstein in the *Tractatus,* though in that same book he had found not only the need but the way to cut himself parially loose from it.

I am still not quite sure why it seems so natural to assume that all words are names, and even that every possible grammatical subject of a sentence, one-worded or many-worded, stands to something as the proper name "Fido" stands to the dog Fido, and, what is a further point, that the thing it stands for is what the expression means. Even Plato had had to fight his way out of the same assumption. But he at least had a special excuse. The Greek language had only the one word ὄνομα where we have the three words "word," "name" and "noun." It was hard in Greek even to say that the Greek counterpart to our verb "is" was a word but not a noun. Greek provided Plato with no label for verbs, or for adverbs, conjunctions etc. That "is" is a word, but is not a name or even a noun was a tricky thing to say in Greek where ὄνομα did duty both for our word "word," for our word "name" and, eventually, for our word "noun." But even without this excuse people still find it natural to assimilate all words to names, and the meanings of words to the bearers of those alleged names. Yet the assumption is easy to demolish.

First, if every single word were a name, then a sentence composed of five words, say "three is a prime number" would be a list of the five objects named by those five words. But a list, like "Plato, Aristotle, Aquinas, Locke, Berkeley" is not a sentence. It says nothing, true or false. A sentence, on the contrary, may say something—some one thing—which is true or false. So the words combined into a sentence at least do something jointly which is different from their severally naming the several things that they name if they do name any things. What a sentence means is not decomposable into the set of things which the words in it stand for, if they do stand for things. So the notion of *having meaning* is at least partly different from the notion of *standing for*.

More than this. I can use the two descriptive phrases "the Morning Star" and "the Evening Star," as different ways of referring to Venus. But it is quite clear that the two phrases are different in meaning. It would be incorrect to translate into French the phrase "the Morning Star" by "l'Étoile du Soir." But if the two phrases have different meanings, then Venus, the planet which we describe by these two different descriptions, cannot be what these descriptive phrases mean. For she, Venus, is one and the same, but what the two phrases signify are different. As we shall see in a moment Mill candidly acknowledges this point and makes an important allowance for it.

Moreover it is easy to coin descriptive phrases to which nothing at all answers. The phrase "the third man to stand on the top of Mt. Everest" cannot, at present, be used to refer to anybody. There exists as yet no one whom it fits and perhaps there never will. Yet it is certainly a significant phrase, and could be translated into French or German. We know, we have to know, what it means when we say that it fits no living mountaineer. It means *something,* but it does not designate *somebody.* What it means cannot, therefore, be equated with a particular mountaineer. Nor can the meaning conveyed by the phrase "the first person to stand on the top of Mt. Everest" be equated with Hillary, though, we gather, it fits him and does not fit anyone else. We can understand the question, and even entertain Nepalese doubts about the answer to the question "Is Hillary the first person to conquer Mt. Everest?" where we could not understand the question "Is Hillary Hillary?"

We could reach the same conclusion even more directly. If Hillary was, *per impossibile,* identified with what is meant by the phrase "the first man to stand on the top of Mt. Everest," it would follow that the meaning of at least one phrase was born in New Zealand, has breathed through an oxygen mask and has been decorated by Her Majesty. But this is patent nonsense. Meanings of phrases are not New Zealand citizens; what is expressed by a particular English phrase, as well as by any paraphrase or translation of it, is not something with lungs, a surname, long legs and a sunburnt face. People are born and die and sometimes wear boots; meanings are not born and do not die and they never wear boots— or go barefoot either. The Queen does not decorate meanings. The phrase "the first man to stand on the top of Mt. Everest" will not lose its meaning when Hillary dies. Nor was it meaningless before he reached the summit.

Finally, we should notice that most words are not nouns; they are, e.g. adverbs, or verbs, or adjectives or prepositions or conjunctions or pronouns. But to classify as a name a word which is not even a noun strikes one as intolerable the moment one considers the point. How could "ran" or "often" or "and" or "pretty" be the name of anything? It could not even be the grammatical subject of a sentence. I may ask what a certain economic condition, moral quality or day of the week is called and get the answer "inflation," "punctiliousness" or "Saturday." We do use the word "name" for what something is called, whether it be what a person or river is called, or what a species, a quality, an action or a condition is called. But the answer to the question "What is it called?" must be a noun or have the grammar of a noun. No such question could be answered by giving the tense of a verb, an adverb, a conjunction or an adjective.

Mill himself allowed that some words like "is," "often," "not," "of," and "the" are not names, even in his hospitable use of "name." They cannot by themselves function as the grammatical subjects of sentences. Their function, as he erroneously described it, is to subserve, in one way or another, the construction of many-worded names. They do not name extra things but are ancillaries to the multi-verbal naming of things. Yet they certainly have meanings. "And" and "or" have different meanings, and "or" and the Latin "aut" have the same meaning. Mill realized that it is not always the case that for a word to mean something, it must denote somebody or some thing. But most of his successors did not notice how important this point was.

Even more to Mill's credit was the fact that he noticed and did partial justice to the point, which I made a little while back, that two different descriptive phrases may both fit the same thing or person, so that the thing or person which they both fit or which, in his unhappy parlance, they both name is not to be equated with either (or of course both) of the significations of the two descriptions. The two phrases "the previous Prime Minister" and "the father of Randolph Churchill" both fit Sir Winston Churchill, and fit only him; but they do not have the same meaning. A French translation of the one would not be a translation of the other. One might know or believe that the one description fitted Sir Winston Churchill while still questioning whether the other did so to. From just knowing that Sir Winston was Prime Minister one could not infer that Randolph Churchill is his son, or vice versa. Either might have been true without the other being true. The two phrases cannot, therefore, carry the same information.

Mill, in effect, met this point with his famous theory of denotation and connotation. Most words and descriptive phrases, according to him, do two things at once. They *denote* the things or persons that they are, as he unhappily puts it, all the names of. But they also *connote* or signify the simple or complex attributes by possessing which the thing or person denoted is fitted by the description. Mill's word "connote" was a very unhappily chosen word and has misled not only Mill's successors but Mill himself. His word "denote" was used by him in a far from uniform way, which left him un-committed to consequences from which some of his successors, who used it less equivocally, could not extricate themselves. For Mill, proper names denote their bearers, but predicate-expressions also denote what they are truly predicable of. Fido is denoted by "Fido" and by "dog" and by "four-legged."

So to ask for the function of an expression is, on Mill's showing, to ask a double question. It is to ask Which person or persons, thing or things the expression denotes? in one or other of Mill's uses of this verb—Sir Winston Churchill, perhaps—, but it is also to ask What are the properties or characteristics by which the thing or person is described?—say that of having begotten Randolph Chur-chill. As a thing or person can be described in various ways, the various descriptions given will differ in connotation, while still being identical in denotation. They characterize in different ways, even though their denotation is identical. They carry different bits of information or misinformation about the same thing, person or event.

Mill himself virtually says that according to our ordinary natural notion of meaning, it would not be proper to say that, e.g. Sir Winston Churchill is the meaning of a word or phrase. We ordi-narily understand by "meaning" not the thing denoted but only what is connoted. That is, Mill virtually reaches the correct con-clusions that the meaning of an expression is never the thing or person referred to by means of it; and that descriptive phrases and, with one exception, single words are never names, in the sense of "proper names." The exception is just those relatively few words which really are proper names, i.e. words like "Fido," and "Lon-don," the words which do not appear in dictionaries.

Mill got a further important point right about these genuine proper names. He said that while most words and descriptive phrases both denote or name and connote, proper names only denote and do not connote. A dog may be called "Fido," but the word "Fido" conveys no information or misinformation about the dog's qualities, career or whereabouts, etc. There is, to enlarge this point, no ques-tion of the word "Fido" being paraphrased, or correctly or incor-rectly translated into French. Dictionaries do not tell us what proper names mean—for the simple reason that they do not mean anything. The word "Fido" names or denotes a particular dog, since it is what he is called. But there is no room for anyone who hears the word "Fido" to understand it or misunderstand it or fail to understand it. There is nothing for which he can require an elucidation or a definition. From the information that Sir Winston Churchill was Prime Minister, a number of consequences follow, such as that he was the leader of the majority party in Parliament. But from the fact that yonder dog is Fido, no other truth about him follows at all. No information is provided for anything to follow from. Using a proper name is not committing oneself to any further assertions whatsoever. Proper names are appellations and not descriptions; and descriptions are descriptions and not appellations. Sir Winston Churchill *is* the father of Randolh Churchill. He is not *called* and was not christened "the father of Randolph Churchill." He is called "Winston Churchill." The Lady Mayoress of Liverpool can give the name *Mauretania* to a ship which thenceforward has that name. But if she called Sir Winston Churchill "the father of Sir Herbert Morrison" this would be a funny sort of christening, but it would not make it true that Morrison is the son of Sir Winston Churchill. Descriptions carry truths or falsehoods and are not just arbitrary bestowals. Proper names are arbitrary bestowals, and convey nothing true and nothing false, for they convey nothing at all.

Chinese astronomers give the planets, stars and constellations names quite different from those we give. But it does not follow that a single proposition of Western astronomy is rejected by them, or that a single astronomical proposition rejected by us is accepted by them. Stellar nomenclature carries with it no astronomical truths or falsehoods. Calling a star by a certain name is not saying anything about it, and saying something true or false about a star is not naming it. Saying is not naming and naming is not saying.

This brings out a most important fact. Considering the meaning (or Mill's "connotation") of an expression is considering what can be said with it, i.e. said truly or said falsely, as well as asked, commanded, advised or any other sort of saying. In this, which is the normal sense of "meaning," the meaning of a sub-expression like a word or phrase, is a functional factor of a range of possible assertions, questions, commands and the rest. It is tributary to sayings. It is a distinguishable common locus of a range of possible tellings, askings, advisings, etc. This precisely inverts the natural assumption with which, as I said earlier, Mill and most of us start, the assumption namely that the meanings of words and phrases can

be learned, discussed and classified before consideration begins of
entire sayings, such as sentences. Word meanings do not stand to
sentence meanings as atoms to molecules or as letters of the alphabet
to the spellings of words, but more nearly as the tennis racket stands
to the strokes which are or may be made with it. This point, which
Mill's successors and predecessors half-recognized to hold for such
little words as "if," "or," "all," "the" and "not," holds good for all
significant words alike. Their significances are their roles inside
actual and possible sayings. Mill's two-way doctrine, that nearly all
words and phrases both denote, or are names, and connote, i.e. have
significance, was therefore, in effect, though unwittingly, a coalition
between an atomistic and a functionalist view of words. By the irony
of fate, it was his atomistic view which was, in most quarters, accepted as gospel truth for the next fifty or seventy years. Indeed, it
was more than accepted, it was accepted without the important safe-
guard which Mill himself provided when he said that the thing or
person denoted by a name was not to be identified with what that
name meant. Mill said that to mean is to connote. His successors
said that to mean is to denote, or, more rarely, both to denote and
to connote. Frege was for a long time alone in seeing the crucial importance of Mill's argument that two or more descriptive phrases
with different senses may apply to the same planet or person. This
person or planet is not, therefore, what those phrases mean. Their
different senses are not their common denotation. Russell early
realized the point which Mill did not very explicitly make, though
Plato had made it, that a sentence is not a list. It says one thing; it is
not just an inventory of a lot of things. But only much later, if at
all, did Russell see the full implications of this.

I surmise that the reason why Mill's doctrine of denotation, without its safeguards, caught on, while his truths about connotation
failed to do so, were two. First, the word "connote" naturally suggests what we express by "imply," which is not what is wanted. What
the phrase "the previous Prime Minister of the United Kingdom"
signifies is not to be equated with any or all of the consequences
which can be inferred from the statement that Churchill is the previous Prime Minister. Deducing is not translating. But more important was the fact that Mill himself rapidly diluted his doctrine
of connotation with such a mass of irrelevant and false sensationa-
list and associationist psychology, that his successors felt forced to
ignore the doctrine in order to keep clear of its accretions.

Let me briefly mention some of the consequences which successors
of Mill actually drew from the view, which was not Mill's, that to

mean is to denote, in the toughest sense, namely that all significant expressions are proper names, and what they are the names of are what the expressions signify.

First, it is obvious that the vast majority of words are unlike the words "Fido" and "London" in this respect, namely, that they are general. "Fido" stands for a particular dog, but the noun "dog" covers this dog Fido, and all other dogs past, present and future, dogs in novels, dogs in dog breeders' plans for the future, and so on indefinitely. So the word "dog," if assumed to denote in the way in which "Fido" denotes Fido, must denote something which we do not hear barking, namely either the set or class of all actual and imaginable dogs, or the set of canine properties which they all share. Either would be a very out-of-the-way sort of entity. Next, most words are not even nouns, but adjectives, verbs, prepositions, conjunctions and so on. If these are assumed to denote in the way in which "Fido" denotes Fido, we shall have a still larger and queerer set of nominees or *denotata* on our hands, namely nominees whose names could not even function as the grammatical subjects of sentences. (Incidentally it is not true even that all ordinary general nouns can function by themselves as subjects of sentences. I can talk about *this* dog, or *a* dog, or *the* dog which . . . ; or about *dogs, all* dogs, or *most* dogs, and so on. But I cannot make the singular noun "dog" by itself the grammatical subject of a sentence, save inside quotes, though I can do this with nouns like "grass," "hydrogen" and "Man"). Finally, since complexes of words, like descriptive and other phrases, and entire clauses and sentences have unitary meanings, then these too will have to be construed as denoting complex entities of very surprising sorts. Now Meinong in Austria and Frege in Germany, as well as Moore and Russell in this country, in their early days, accepted some or most of these consequences. Consistently with the assumed equation of signifying with naming, they maintained the objective existence of being of all sorts of abstract and fictional *entia rationis*.

Whenever we construct a sentence, in which we can distinguish a grammatical subject and a verb, the grammatical subject, be it a single word or a more or less complex phrase, must be significant if the sentence is to say something true or false. But if this nominative word or phrase is significant, it must, according to the assumption, denote something which is there to be named. So not only Fido and London, but also centaurs, round squares, the present King of France, the class of albino Cypriots, the first moment of time, and the nonexistence of a first moment of time must all be credited with some sort of reality. They must *be,* else we could not say true or false things of them. We could not truly say that round squares do not exist, unless in some sense of "exist" there exist round squares for us, in another sense, to deny existence of. Sentences can begin with abstract nouns like "equality" or "justice" or "murder" so all Plato's Forms or Universals must be accepted as entities. Sentences can contain mentions of creatures of fiction, like centaurs and Mr. Pickwick, so all conceivable creatures of fiction must be genuine entities too. Next, we can say that propositions are true or false, or that they entail or are incompatible with other propositions, so any significant "that"-clause, like "that three is a prime number" or "that four is a prime number," must also denote existent or subsistent objects. It was accordingly, for a time, supposed that if I know or believe that three is a prime number, my knowing or believing this is a special relation holding between me on the one hand and the truth or fact, on the other, denoted by the sentence "three is a prime number." If I weave or follow a romance, my imagining centaurs or Mr. Pickwick is a special relation holding between me and these centaurs or that portly old gentleman. I could not imagine him unless he had enough being to stand as the correlate-term in this postulated relation of being imagined by me.

Lastly, to consider briefly what turned out, unexpectedly, to be a crucial case, there must exist or subsist classes, namely appropriate *denotata* for such collectively employed plural descriptive phrases as "the elephants in Burma" or "the men in the moon." It is just of such classes or sets that we say that they number 3000, say, in the one case, and 0 in the other. For the results of counting to be true or false, there must be entities submitting to numerical predicates; and for the propositions of arithmetic to be true or false there must exist or subsist an infinite range of such classes.

At the very beginning of this century Russell was detecting some local unplausibilities in the full-fledged doctrine that to every significant grammatical subject there must correspond an appropriate *denotatum* in the way in which Fido answers to the name "Fido." The true proposition "round squares do not exist" surely cannot require us to assert that there really do subsist round squares. The proposition that it is false that four is a prime number is a true one, but its truth surely cannot force us to fill the Universe up with an endless population of objectively existing falsehoods.

But it was classes that first engendered not mere unplausibilities but seemingly disastrous logical contradictions—not merely peripheral logical contradictions but contradictions at the heart of the

very principles on which Russell and Frege had taken mathematics
to depend. We can collect into classes not only ordinary objects like
playing-cards and bachelors, but also such things as classes themselves. I can ask how many shoes there are in a room and also how
many pairs of shoes, and a pair of shoes is already a class. So now
suppose I construct a class of all the classes that are not, as anyhow
most classes are not, members of themselves. Will this class be one of
its own members or not? If it embraces itself, this disqualifies it from
being one of the things it is characterized as embracing; if it is not
one of the things it embraces, this is just what qualifies it to be one
among its own members.

So simple logic itself forbids certain ostensibly denoting expressions to denote. It is at least unplausible to say that there exist
objects denoted by the phrase "round squares"; there is self-contra-
diction in saying that there exists a class which is a member of itself
on condition that it is not, and vice versa.

Russell had already found himself forced to say of some expressions which had previously been supposed to name or denote, that
they had to be given exceptional treatment. They were not names
but what he called "incomplete symbols," expressions, that is, which
have no meaning, in the sense of denotation, by themselves; their
business was to be auxiliary to expressions which do, as a whole,
denote. (This was what Mill had said of the syncategorematic
words.) The very treatment which had since the Middle Ages been
given to such little words as "and," "not," "the," "some" and "is"
was not given to some other kinds of expressions as well. In effect,
though not explicitly, Russell was saying that, e.g. descriptive
phrases were as syncategorematic as "not," "and" and "is" had always
been allowed to be. Here Russell was on the brink of allowing that
the meanings of significations of many kinds of expressions are
matters not of *naming* things, but of *saying* things. But he was, I
think, still held up by the idea that saying is itself just another
variety of naming, i.e. naming a complex or an "objective" or a
proposition or a fact—some sort of postulated *Fido rationis*.

He took a new and most important further step to cope with the
paradoxes, like that of the class of classes that are not members of
themselves. For he now wielded a distinction, which Mill had seen
but left inert, the distinction between sentences which are either
true or false on the one hand, and on the other hand sentences
which, though proper in vocabulary and syntax, are none the less
nonsensical, meaningless or absurd; and therefore neither true nor
false. To assert them and to deny them are to assert and deny

nothing. For reasons of a sort which are the proper concern of logic, certain sorts of concatenations of words and phrases into sentences produce things which cannot be significantly said. For example, the very question Is the class of all classes which are not members of themselves a member of itself or not? has no answer. Russell's famous "Theory of Types" was an attempt to formulate the reasons of logic which make it an improper question. We need not consider whether he was successful. What matters for us, and what made the big difference to subsequent philosophy, is the fact that at long last the notion of meaning was realized to be, at least in certain crucial contexts, the obverse of the notion of the nonsensical—what can be said, truly or falsely, is at last contrasted with what cannot be significantly said. The notion of meaning had been, at long last, partly detached from the notion of naming and re-attached to the notion of saying. It was recognized to belong to, or even to constitute the domain which had always been the province of logic; and as it is at least part of the official business of logic to establish and codify rules, the notion of meaning came now to be seen as somehow compact of rules. To know what an expression means involves knowing what can (logically) be said with it and what cannot (logically) be said with it. It involves knowing a set of bans, fiats and obligations, or, in a word, it is to know the rules of the employment of that expression.

It was, however, not Russell but Wittgenstein who first generalized or half-generalized this crucial point. In the *Tractatus Logico-Philosophicus,* which could be described as the first book to be written on the philosophy of logic, Wittgenstein still had one foot in the denotationist camp, but his other foot was already free. He saw and said, not only what had been said before, that the little words, the so-called logical constants, "not," "is," "and" and the rest do not stand for objects, but also, what Plato had also said before, that sentences are not names. Saying is not naming. He realized, as Frege had done, that logicians' questions are not questions about the properties or relations of the *denotata,* if any, of the expressions which enter into the sentences whose logic is under examination. He saw, too, that all the words and phrases that can enter into sentences are governed by the rules of what he called, slightly metaphorically, "logical syntax" or "logical grammar." These rules are what are broken by such concatenations of words and phrases as result in nonsense. Logic is or includes the study of these rules. Husserl had at the beginning of the century employed much the same notion of "logical grammar."

It was only later still that Wittgenstein consciously and deliberately withdrew his remaining foot from the denotationist camp.
When he said "Don't ask for the meaning, ask for the use," he was
imparting a lesson which he had had to teach to himself after he had
finished with the *Tractatus*. The use of an expression, or the concept it expresses, is the role it is employed to perform, not any thing
or person or event for which it might be supposed to stand. Nor is
the purchasing power of a coin to be equated with this book or that
car ride which might be bought with it. The purchasing power of
a coin has not got pages or a terminus. Even more instructive is the
analogy which Wittgenstein now came to draw between significant
expressions and the pieces with which are played games like chess.
The significance of an expression and the powers or functions in
chess of a pawn, a knight or the queen have much in common. To
know what the knight can and cannot do, one must know the rules
of chess, as well as be familiar with various kinds of chess situations
which may arise. What the knight may do cannot be read out of the
material or shape of the piece of ivory or boxwood or tin of which
this knight may be made. Similarly to know what an expression
means is to know how it may and may not be employed, and the
rules governing its employment can be the same for expressions of
very different physical compositions. The word "horse" is not a bit
like the word "cheval"; but the way of wielding them is the same.
They have the same role, the same sense. Each is a translation of the
other. Certainly the rules of the uses of expressions are unlike the
rules of games in some important respects. We can be taught the
rules of chess up to a point before we begin to play. There are
manuals of chess, where there are not manuals of significance. The
rules of chess, again, are completely definite and inelastic. Questions
of whether a rule has been broken or not are decidable without
debate. Moreover we opt to play chess and can stop when we like,
where we do not opt to talk and think and cannot opt to break off.
Chess is a diversion. Speech and thought are not only diversions.
But still the partial assimilation of the meanings of expressions to
the powers or the values of the pieces with which a game is played
is enormously revealing. There is no temptation to suppose that a
knight is proxy for anything, or that learning what a knight may or
may not do is learning that it is a deputy for some ulterior entity.
We could not learn to play the knight correctly without having
learned to play the other pieces, nor can we learn to play a word by
itself, but only in combination with other words and phrases.

Besides this, there is a further point which the assimilation brings out. There are six different kinds of chess pieces, with their six different kinds of roles in the game. We can imagine more complex games involving twenty or two hundred kinds of pieces. So it is with languages. In contrast with the denotationist assumption that almost all words, all phrases and even all sentences are alike in having the one role of naming, the assimilation of language to chess reminds us of what we knew *ambulando* all along, the fact that there are indefinitely many kinds of words, kinds of phrases, and kinds of sentences—that there is an indefinitely large variety of kinds of roles performed by the expressions we use in saying things. Adjectives do not do what adverbs do, nor do all adjectives do the same sort of thing as one another. Some nouns are proper names, but most are not. The sorts of things that we do with sentences are different from the sorts of things that we do with most single words—and some sorts of things that we can significantly do with some sorts of sentences, we cannot significantly do with others. And so on.

There is not one basic mold, such as the "Fido"-Fido mold, into which all significant expressions are to be forced. On the contrary, there is an endless variety of categories of sense or meaning. Even the *prima facie* simple notion of naming or denoting itself turns out on examination to be full of internal variegations. Pronouns are used to denote people and things, but not in the way in which proper names do so. No one is *called* "he" or "she." "Saturday" is a proper name, but not in the same way as "Fido" is a proper name —and neither is used in the way in which the fictional proper name "Mr. Pickwick" is used. The notion of denotation, so far from providing the final explanation of the notion of meaning, turns out itself to be just one special branch or twig on the tree of signification. Expressions do not mean because they denote things; some expressions denote things, in one or another of several different manners, because they are significant. Meanings are not things, not even very queer things. Learning the meaning of an expression is more like learning a piece of drill than like coming across a previously unencountered object. It is learning to operate correctly with an expression and with any other expression equivalent to it.

The Theory of Philosophy

I now want to trace, rather more cursorily, the other main motive from which thinkers have posed the abstract question What are meanings? or What is it for an expression to have a certain sense? Until fairly recently philosophers have not often stepped back from their easels to consider what philosophy is, or how doing philosophy differs from doing science, or doing theology, or doing mathematics. Kant was the first modern thinker to see or try to answer this question—and a very good beginning of an answer he gave; but I shall not expound his answer here.

This question did not begin seriously to worry the general run of philosophers until maybe sixty years ago. It began to become obsessive only after the publication of the *Tractatus*. Why did the philosophy of philosophy start so late, and how did it come to start when and as it did?

It is often not realized that the words "philosophy" and "philosopher" and their equivalents in French and German had for a long time much less specific meanings than they now possess. During the seventeenth, the eighteenth and most of the nineteenth centuries a "philosopher" was almost any sort of a *savant*. Astronomers, chemists and botanists were called "philosophers" just as much as were Locke, Berkeley or Hume. Descartes' philosophy covered his contributions to optics just as much as his contributions to epistemology. In English there existed for a long time no special word for the people we now call "scientists." This noun was deliberately coined only in 1840, and even then it took some time to catch on. His contemporaries could not call Newton a "scientist," since there was no such word. When a distinction had to be made, it was made by distinguishing "natural philosophy" from "moral" and "metaphysical philosophy." As late as 1887, Conan Doyle, within two or three pages of one story, describes Sherlock Holmes as being totally ignorant of philosophy, as we use the word now, and yet as having his room full of philosophical, i.e. scientific, instruments, like test tubes, retorts and balances. A not very ancient Oxford Chair of Physics still retains its old label, the Chair of Experimental Philosophy.

Different from this quite important piece of etymological history is the fact that both in Scotland and in England there existed from perhaps the time of Hartley to that of Sidgwick and Bradley a strong tendency to suppose that the distinction between natural philosophy, i.e. physical and biological science on the one hand and metaphysical and moral philosophy, perhaps including logic, on the other, was that the latter were concerned with internal, mental phenomena, where the former were concerned with external, physical phenomena. Much of what we now label "philosophy," *sans phrase*, was for a long time and by many thinkers confidently, but quite wrongly equated with what we now call "psychology." John Stuart Mill sometimes, but not always, uses even the grand word "metaphysics" for

the empirical study of the workings of men's minds. Protests were
made against this equation particularly on behalf of philosophical
theology, but for a long time the antitheologians had it their own
way. A philosopher, *sans phrase,* was a Mental and Moral Scientist
—a scientist who was exempted from working in the laboratory or
the observatory only because his specimens were collected at home
by introspection. Even Mansel, himself a philosophical theologian
with a good Kantian equipment, maintained that the science of
mental phenomena, what we call "psychology," was the real basis
of even ontological or theological speculations.

So not only did the wide coverage of the word "philosophy" en-
courage people not to look for any important differences between
what scientists, as we now call them, do and what philosophers, as
we now call them, do; but even when such differences were looked
for, they were apt to be found in the differences between the investigation of physical phenomena by the laboratory scientist and the
investigation of psychological phenomena by the introspecting
psychologist.

As I see it, three influences were chiefly responsible for the collapse of the assumption that doing philosophy, in our sense, is of a
piece with doing natural science or at least of a piece with doing
mental science or psychology.

First, champions of mathematics like Frege, Husserl, and Russell
had to save mathematics from the combined empiricism and psy-
chologism of the school of John Stuart Mill. Mathematical truths
are not mere psychological generalizations; equations are not mere
records of deeply rutted associations of ideas; the objects of geome-
try are not of the stuff of which mental images are made. Pure
mathematics is a noninductive and a nonintrospective science. Its
proofs are rigorous, its terms are exact, and its theorems are universal and not merely highly general truths. The proofs and the theorems of Formal or Symbolic Logic share these dignities with the
proofs and theorems of mathematics. So, as logic was certainly a part
of philosophy, not all of philosophy could be ranked as "mental
science." There must, then, be a field of realm besides those of the
material and the mental; and at least part of philosophy is concerned
with this third realm, the realm of nonmaterial and also nonmental
"logical objects"—such objects as concepts, truths, falsehoods, classes,
numbers and implications.

Next, armchair mental science or introspective psychology itself
began to yield ground to experimental, laboratory psychology. Psychologists like James began to put themselves to school under the

physiologists and the statisticians. Scientific psychology began first to rival and then to oust both a priori and introspective psychology, and the tacit claim of epistemologists, moral philosophers and logicians to be mental scientists had to be surrendered to those who used the methods and the tools of the reputable sciences. So the question raised its head. What then were the objects of the inquiries of epistemologists, moral philosophers and logicians, if they were not, as had been supposed, psychological states and processes? It is only in our own days that, anyhow in most British Universities, psychologists have established a Faculty of their own separate from the Faculty of Philosophy.

Thirdly, Brentano, reinforcing from medieval sources a point made and swiftly forgotten by Mill, maintained as an a priori principle of psychology itself, that it is of the essence of mental states and processes that they are *of* objects or contents. Somewhat as in grammar a transitive verb requires an accusative, so in the field of ideas, thoughts and feelings, acts of consciousness are directed upon their own metaphorical accusatives. To see is to see something, to regret is to regret something, to conclude or suppose is to conclude or suppose that something is the case. Imagining is one thing, the thing imagined, a centaur, say, is another. The centaur has the body of a horse and does not exist. An act of imagining a centaur does exist and does not have the body of a horse. Your act of supposing that Napoleon defeated Wellington is different from my act of supposing it; but what we suppose is the same and is what is expressed by our common expression "that Napoleon defeated Wellington." What is true of mental acts is, in general, false of their accusatives or "intentional objects," and vice versa.

Brentano's two pupils, Meinong and Husserl, happened, for different reasons, to be especially, though not exclusively, interested in applying this principle of intentionality or transitivity to the intellectual, as distinct from the sensitive, volitional or affective acts of consciousness. They set out, that is, to rectify the Locke-Hume-Mill accounts of abstraction, conception, memory, judgment, supposal, inference and the rest, by distinguishing in each case, the various private, momentary and repeatable acts of conceiving, remembering, judging, supposing and inferring from their public, nonmomentary accusatives, namely, the concepts, the propositions and the implications which constituted their objective correlates. Where Frege attacked psychologistic accounts of thinking from the outside, they attacked them from the inside. Where Frege argued, for instance, that numbers have nothing psychological or, of course, physical about them, Husserl and Meinong argued that for the mental processes of counting and calculating to be what they are, they must have accusatives or objects numerically and qualitatively other than those processes themselves. Frege said that Mill's account of mathematical entities was false because psychological; Husserl and Meinong, in effect, said that the psychology itself was false because non-"intentional" psychology. The upshot, however, was much the same. With different axes to grind, all three came to what I may crudely dub "Platonistic" conclusions. All three maintained the doctrine of a third realm of nonphysical, nonpsychological entities, in which realm dwelled such things as concepts, numbers, classes and propositions.

Husserl and Meinong were both ready to lump together all these accusatives of thinking alike under the comprehensive title of Meanings (*Bedeutungen*), since what I think is what is conveyed by the words, phrases or sentences in which I express what I think. The "accusatives" of my ideas and my judgings are the meanings of my words and my sentences. It easily followed from this that both Husserl and Meinong, proud of their newly segregated third realm, found that it was this realm which provided a desiderated subject matter peculiar to logic and philosophy and necessarily ignored by the natural sciences, physical and psychological. Mental acts and states are the subject matter of psychology. Physical objects and events are the subject matter of the physical and biological sciences. It is left to philosophy to be the science of this third domain which consists largely, though not entirely, of thought objects or Meanings—the novel and impressive entities which had been newly isolated for separate investigation by the application of Brentano's principle of intentionality to the specifically intellectual or cognitive acts of consciousness.

Thus, by the first decade of this century it was dawning upon philosophers and logicians that their business was not that of one science among others, e.g. that of psychology; and even that it was not an inductive, experimental or observational business of any sort. It was intimately concerned with, among other things, the fundamental concepts and principles of mathematics; and it seemed to have to do with a special domain which was not bespoken by any other discipline, namely the so-called third realm of logical objects or Meanings. At the same time, and in some degree affected by these influences, Moore consistently and Russell spasmodically were prosecuting their obviously philosophical and logical inquiries with a special *modus operandi*. They, and not they alone, were deliberately

and explicitly trying to give analyses of concepts and propositions
—asking What does it really mean to say, for example, that this is
good? or that that is true? or that centaurs do not exist? or that I
see an inkpot? or What are the differences between the distinguishable senses of the verb "to know" and the verb "to be"? Moore's
regular practice and Russell's frequent practice seemed to exemplify
beautifully what, for example, Husserl and Meinong had declared
in general terms to be the peculiar business of philosophy and logic,
namely to explore the third realm of Meanings. Thus philosophy
had acquired a right to live its own life, neither as a discredited
pretender to the status of the science of mind, not yet as a superan-
nuated handmaiden of démodé theology. It was responsible for a
special field of facts, facts of impressively Platonized kinds.

Before the first world war discussions of the status and role of
philosophy vis-à-vis the mathematical and empirical sciences were
generally cursory and incidental to discussions of other matters.
Wittgenstein's *Tractatus* was a complete treatise dedicated to fixing
the position mainly of Formal Logic but also, as a necessary corollary, the position of general philosophy. It was this book which
made dominant issues of the theory of logic and the theory of philosophy. In Vienna some of its teachings were applied polemically,
namely to demolishing the pretensions of philosophy to be the science of transcendent realities. In England, on the whole, others of
its teachings were applied more constructively, namely to stating
the positive functions which philosophical propositions perform,
and scientific propositions do not perform. In England, on the whole,
interest was concentrated on Wittgenstein's description of philosophy as an activity of clarifying or elucidating the meanings of the
expressions used, e.g. by scientists; that is, on the medicinal virtues of
his account of the nonsensical. In Vienna, on the whole, interest was
concentrated on the lethal potentialities of Wittgenstein's account
of nonsense. In both places, it was realized that the criteria between
the significant and the nonsensical needed to be systematically sur-
veyed, and that it was for the philosopher and not the scientist to
survey them.

At this point, the collapse of the denotationist theory of meaning
began to influence the theory of philosophy as the science of Platonized Meanings. If the meaning of an expression is not an entity
denoted by it, but a style of operation performed with it, not a
nominee but a role, then it is not only repellent but positively misleading to speak as if there existed a Third Realm whose denizens
are Meanings. We can distinguish this knight, as a piece of ivory,

from the part it or any proxy for it may play in a game of chess; but
the part it may play is not an extra entity, made of some mysterious
nonivory. There is not one box housing the ivory chessmen and another queerer box housing their functions in chess games. Similarly
we can distinguish an expression as a set of syllables from its employment. A quite different set of syllables may have the same employment. But its use or sense is not an additional substance or subject of predication. It is not a nonphysical, nonmental object—but
not because it is either a physical or a mental object, but because it
is not an object. As it is not an object, it is not a denizen of a
Platonic realm of objects. To say, therefore, that philosophy is the
science of Meanings, though not altogether wrong, is liable to mislead in the same way as it might mislead to say that economics is the
science of exchange-values. This, too, is true enough, but to word
this truth in this way is liable to make people suppose that the Universe houses, under different roofs, commodities and coins here and
exchange-values over there.

Hence, following Wittgenstein's lead, it has become customary
to say, instead, that philosophical problems are linguistic problems
—only linguistic problems quite unlike any of the problems of
philology, grammar, phonetics, rhetoric, prosody, etc., since they
are problems about the logic of the functionings of expressions.
Such problems are so widely different from, e.g. philological problems, that speaking of them as linguistic problems is, at the moment,
as Wittgenstein foresaw, misleading people as far in one direction,
as speaking of them as problems about Meanings or Concepts or
Propositions had been misleading in the other direction. The difficulty is to steer between the Scylla of a Platonistic and the Charyb-
dis of a lexicographical account of the business of philosophy and
logic.

There has been and perhaps still is something of a vogue for saying
that doing philosophy consists in analyzing meanings, or analyzing
the employments of expressions. Indeed, from Transatlantic journals
I gather that at this very moment British philosophy is dominated
by some people called "linguistic analysts." The word "analysis"
has, indeed, a good laboratory or Scotland Yard ring about it; it
contrasts well with such expressions as "speculation," "hypothesis,"
"system-building" and even "preaching" and "writing poetry." On
the other hand it is a hopelessly misleading word in some important
respects. It falsely suggests, for one thing, that any sort of careful
elucidation of any sorts of complex or subtle ideas will be a piece
of philosophizing; as if the judge, in explaining to the members of

the jury the differences between manslaughter and murder, was helping them out of a philosophical quandary. But, even worse, it suggests that philosophical problems are like the chemist's or the detective's problems in this respect, namely that they can and should be tackled piecemeal. Finish problem A this morning, file the answer, and go on to problem B this afternoon. This suggestion does violence to the vital fact that philosophical problems inevitably interlock in all sorts of ways. It would be patently absurd to tell someone to finish the problem of the nature of truth this morning, file the answer and go on this afternoon to solve the problem of the relations between naming and saying, holding over until tomorrow problems about the concepts of existence and nonexistence. This is, I think, why at the present moment philosophers are far more inclined to liken their task to that of the cartographer than to that of the chemist or the detective. It is the foreign relations, not the domestic constitutions of sayables that engender logical troubles and demand logical arbitration.

ABOUT THE AUTHORS

ARTHUR OWEN BARFIELD (1898-   ) is a solicitor, whose studies in language and literature have resulted in many essays and a number of notable books, among them *Poetic Diction* (1952) and *Saving the Appearances* (1957).

SAMUEL BUTLER (1835-1902) was a greatly talented and stimulatingly eccentric Victorian, whose many accomplishments included painting, musical criticism, and a characteristically heterodox appraisal of Darwinian theory. Of his many books, the great satire, *Erewhon* (1872), is as fresh as on the day it was written and his posthumous novel, *The Way of All Flesh* (1903), a savage and hilarious exploration of family relations, would suffice to preserve his reputation as a great writer.

WALTER BRYCE GALLIE (1912-   ) has been a Professor of Logic and Metaphysics at the Queen's University of Belfast since 1954. His many writings on philosophy and education include a valuable introduction to pragmatism, entitled *Peirce and Pragmatism* (Pelican Books, 1952).

ALDOUS HUXLEY (1894-1963) has been too well-known a writer to need an introduction. The long list of his writings includes the memorable novels *Point Counter Point* (1928), *Brave New World* (1932), and many other stories and essays which have enriched the intellectual life of his time.

CLIVE STAPLES LEWIS (1898-1963) has been Professor of Medieval and Renaissance English at Cambridge University. He has written books such as *The Allegory of Love* (1936) that are highly regarded by specialists, provocative discussions of Christian theology, like his famous *The Screwtape Letters* (1942), distinguished science fiction such as *Perelandra* (1943) and several children's books. His *Studies of Words* (1960) would interest the reader of the present collection.

BRONISLAW KASPER MALINOWSKI (1884-1942) was a Polish born anthropologist who settled in England. As a Professor of Social Anthropology at the London School of Economics, he exerted great influence through his "functional" theories of culture and society. His *Sex and Repression in Savage Society* (1927) is possibly his best known book.

ALAN STRODE CAMPBELL ROSS (1907-   ) has been Professor of Linguistics at Birmingham University since 1951. An expert in English and Germanic philology, he has written *The Terfinnas and Beormas of Othere* (1940) and other studies equally inaccessible to the layman. His famous paper, "U and Non-U," which showed him to have a keenly satirical eye for class distinctions as reflected in speech, aroused lively and prolonged discussion in England. He can claim to have added the expression "non-U" to the English language as now spoken.

GILBERT RYLE (1900-   ) has been Waynflete Professor of Metaphysical Philosophy in the University of Oxford. His book *The Concept of Mind* (1949) has been one of the most widely discussed of all twentieth century philosophical works.

FRIEDRICH WAISMANN (1896-1959) was born in Vienna, trained as a mathematician and philosopher and was later closely associated with the famous group of scientists and philosophers known as "The Vienna Circle." On taking refuge in England in 1937 he first taught at Cambridge and two years later became Reader in the Philosophy of Mathematics at the University of Oxford, a post he held until his death. In addition to many papers, he wrote *Introduction to Mathematical Thinking* (1951).

MAX BLACK (1909-   ) is a past President of the American Philosophical Association, a Fellow of the American Academy of Arts and Sciences, and a member of the International Institute of Philosophy. Well-known for numerous publications, among them: *Critical Thinking, The Nature of Mathematics, Language and Philosophy, Problems of Analysis, Models and Metaphors, A Companion to Wittgenstein's* Tractatus, *The Labyrinth of Language,* and (editor) *Philosophy in America,* Professor Black is Susan Linn Sage Professor of Philosophy and Director of the Society for the Humanities at Cornell University.